Building Real-Time Web Apps with Node.js: Create Scalable Apps

A Complete Guide to Developing Real-Time Applications with Node.js

BOOZMAN RICHARD

BOOKER BLUNT

Table of Content

TABLE OF CONTENTS

INTRODUCTION

In today's fast-paced digital landscape, the demand for real-time, interactive web applications has never been greater. Whether it's messaging, live updates, collaborative tools, or real-time data streaming, users expect instantaneous interactions with minimal latency. From chat applications and online gaming to live streaming services and financial trading platforms, real-time web apps are revolutionizing the way we interact with the internet.

Building real-time applications, however, comes with its own set of challenges. Unlike traditional web applications that rely on synchronous request-response cycles, real-time web apps demand asynchronous communication, constant connection persistence, and seamless scalability. They require a deep understanding of technologies like WebSockets, message queues, event-driven architecture, and real-time data processing.

This book, **"Building Real-Time Web Apps with Node.js: Create Scalable Apps,"** is designed to guide you through the process of developing efficient, scalable, and high-performance real-time applications using **Node.js**. Whether you're a beginner looking to explore real-time development or an experienced developer seeking to sharpen your skills, this book offers practical, hands-on insights into building real-time apps that respond instantly to user actions, process live data, and scale seamlessly.

7

Why Real-Time Web Apps?

The power of real-time communication lies in its ability to provide users with instantaneous feedback and interaction. Traditional web applications were built on an **HTTP request-response model,** where a client would send a request to the server, and the server would respond with the requested data. While this works well for many types of applications, it becomes inefficient when you need to push live data or interactions to users, such as when someone sends a message in a chat or places a bid in an auction.

In contrast, real-time web applications allow clients to establish **persistent connections** with the server, which can push data to clients in real time. This allows for instant notifications, live updates, and bidirectional communication between the client and server.

Examples of real-time applications include:

- **Messaging apps**: Instant chat applications like WhatsApp or Slack that provide real-time communication.
- **Social media platforms**: Apps like Twitter or Facebook where you get live updates of your feed.
- **Live streaming services**: Platforms like Twitch or YouTube Live that allow users to watch events or broadcasts in real time.

- **Collaborative tools**: Real-time document editing apps like Google Docs where multiple users can edit a document simultaneously.

- **Financial trading apps**: Real-time stock trading platforms that display live market data and allow for immediate trade execution.

The need for real-time applications has exploded in recent years, driven by the rise of mobile technology, social media, and the increasing expectation of instantaneous information.

The Role of Node.js in Real-Time Development

Node.js, with its non-blocking, event-driven architecture, has become the ideal platform for building real-time web apps. Unlike traditional server-side technologies that rely on a thread-per-request model, Node.js utilizes a **single-threaded event loop**, making it incredibly efficient at handling large numbers of concurrent connections. This makes Node.js perfect for applications that require real-time data processing and communication.

Here's why Node.js is a game-changer for real-time app development:

- **Asynchronous, Non-blocking I/O:** Node.js can handle many concurrent connections without blocking the event loop, which is crucial for real-time apps that require frequent data exchanges.

- **Scalability:** Node.js supports horizontal scaling, meaning it can handle growing numbers of users and high traffic with minimal performance degradation.

- **Rich Ecosystem:** With a vast ecosystem of **npm (Node Package Manager)** modules, Node.js offers powerful libraries for implementing real-time features like WebSockets, message queues, and server-side events.

- **Low Latency:** Node.js provides low-latency communication, making it ideal for applications that require fast updates, like gaming, chat, and live streaming.

- **JavaScript Everywhere:** Node.js allows you to use JavaScript both on the server-side and client-side, streamlining development processes and enabling a uniform development stack.

With these advantages, Node.js has become the go-to solution for developers looking to build scalable and efficient real-time web applications.

What You Will Learn in This Book

This book takes you on a journey through the essential concepts and practical implementations needed to build real-time applications using Node.js. We start with foundational topics and move towards more advanced real-time features, giving you a thorough understanding of how to handle real-time communication, optimize for performance, and scale your apps.

Here's what you can expect to learn:

1. **Foundations of Real-Time Web Apps**:
   - You'll start by understanding the key principles of real-time communication and why traditional HTTP isn't sufficient for these types of applications.
   - We'll introduce core concepts like **WebSockets**, **REST APIs**, and **HTTP/2**, and explain how they fit into the real-time architecture.

2. **Setting Up a Real-Time Backend with Node.js**:
   - We'll guide you through building a Node.js server capable of handling real-time interactions. You'll learn how to use **Socket.IO** and **WebSockets** to establish persistent, low-latency connections between clients and the server.
   - We'll cover how to secure WebSocket connections using **WSS** (WebSocket Secure) and implement authentication with **JWT (JSON Web Tokens)**.

3. **Scaling Real-Time Apps**:
   - As real-time apps grow, they must scale to handle more users and higher traffic. This book will

teach you how to scale your applications effectively using techniques like load balancing, clustering, and **horizontal scaling** with Node.js.

o You'll learn how to manage state and handle event-driven architectures using tools like **Redis** and **Kafka** for **pub/sub messaging**.

4. **Building Advanced Real-Time Features**:

o We will dive deep into real-time features like **video and audio streaming** using **WebRTC** and **live notifications** for mobile and desktop apps.

o You'll also explore how to implement real-time collaboration features, such as collaborative document editing, using event-driven programming and real-time data synchronization.

5. **Security, Monitoring, and Deployment**:

o Securing real-time apps is critical. We'll show you how to protect your app from security vulnerabilities like **DoS/DDoS attacks**, **data breaches**, and **session hijacking**.

o You'll also learn how to monitor and troubleshoot real-time apps using **logging**, **metrics**, and **dashboards**, and how to deploy your applications using **Docker**, **Kubernetes**, and cloud platforms like **AWS**.

6. **Real-World Examples**:

o Throughout the book, we provide practical, real-world examples. You'll create a **real-time messaging app** from scratch and integrate advanced features like **push notifications**, **message queues**, and **AI-powered recommendations**.

Who This Book Is For

This book is designed for developers who are eager to learn how to build **real-time web applications** with Node.js. Whether you're a beginner just starting with web development or an experienced developer looking to learn how to leverage the power of real-time technologies, this book has something for you.

- **Beginners**: If you're new to real-time web development or Node.js, this book starts with the basics, building your understanding of key concepts and progressively guiding you to more advanced topics.
- **Intermediate Developers**: If you already have experience with Node.js and want to specialize in real-time applications, this book will help you apply your knowledge to create highly interactive and scalable apps.
- **Advanced Developers**: For experienced developers, this book provides practical insights into **scalability, security,**

and **optimization**, along with real-world examples of building and deploying complex real-time apps.

Conclusion

Building real-time web applications is an exciting and rewarding challenge that opens up new opportunities for creating interactive, engaging, and dynamic user experiences. With **Node.js** as the backbone of your app, you can easily manage thousands of concurrent connections and deliver instant updates to users.

This book is your comprehensive guide to mastering real-time application development using Node.js. You'll go from building basic real-time apps to handling complex features like video streaming, real-time messaging, and scalable architecture. By the end of this book, you'll have the knowledge and skills to build your own robust, scalable real-time web applications and bring your ideas to life.

Let's begin your journey into the world of real-time web development with Node.js!

CHAPTER 1

INTRODUCTION TO REAL-TIME WEB APPS AND NODE.JS

Overview of Real-Time Web Apps

Real-time web applications are platforms that allow continuous, instantaneous interaction between users or systems. Unlike traditional web apps that rely on users sending requests and waiting for responses, real-time web apps facilitate continuous communication between the client and server. This makes them ideal for applications like chat platforms, live notifications, online gaming, and collaborative tools.

In real-time apps, data is instantly updated without requiring the user to refresh the page, creating a smooth, interactive experience. Real-time apps leverage technologies that enable two-way communication between the client (browser) and server. A good example of a real-time web app is a live chat application, where users can send and receive messages instantly without waiting for a server request.

Common characteristics of real-time web apps include:

- **Instantaneous communication:** Information is pushed to the client as soon as it's available.
- **Interactive user experience:** Users are actively engaged in real-time without delay.
- **Continuous server communication:** The server keeps an open connection with the client to send updates continuously.

Examples of real-time web apps:

- **Messaging apps**: WhatsApp, Facebook Messenger
- **Collaboration tools**: Google Docs (for live document editing)
- **Live sports scores or stock tickers**: Apps that update in real-time with live data
- **Online games**: Multiplayer games where players interact in real-time

These applications are powered by technologies like WebSockets, HTTP/2, and server-sent events, which we will explore in this book.

Why Node.js is Ideal for Real-Time Applications

Node.js is an open-source, server-side JavaScript runtime built on Chrome's V8 engine. It is designed to build scalable network applications, and its event-driven, non-blocking I/O model makes it particularly suited for real-time applications.

Here are several reasons why Node.js is perfect for building real-time web apps:

1. **Asynchronous and Non-blocking I/O:** Node.js uses an event-driven, non-blocking I/O model, meaning it can handle multiple requests simultaneously without waiting for each one to complete before moving to the next. This feature is crucial for real-time apps that need to manage a large number of simultaneous connections.

2. **Single-threaded Event Loop:** Unlike traditional multi-threaded models, Node.js uses a single-threaded event loop to handle all requests. This reduces overhead and makes it lightweight and efficient for handling numerous real-time requests.

3. **Fast Performance:** Node.js is built on the V8 JavaScript engine, which compiles JavaScript directly into machine code. This ensures high performance, which is critical for real-time applications requiring low-latency responses.

4. **Scalability:** Node.js can easily handle numerous concurrent connections with minimal overhead. As real-time applications often involve handling multiple users or requests at the same time, Node.js's ability to scale horizontally (adding more instances to the server) makes it ideal for large-scale applications.

5. **Large Ecosystem of Libraries and Tools:** Node.js has an extensive ecosystem of open-source libraries (thanks to npm, Node's package manager) that makes it easier to integrate additional functionality into your real-time apps, such as WebSocket libraries, authentication, database connectors, and much more.

6. **Unified Language for Server and Client:** Since Node.js is built on JavaScript, you can use JavaScript on both the client-side and server-side of your real-time application. This consistency simplifies development and allows developers to work in one language throughout the entire stack.

Setting Up a Node.js Development Environment

To get started with building real-time web apps using Node.js, you need to set up your development environment. Here's a step-by-step guide:

1. **Install Node.js:**
   o Go to the official Node.js website and download the latest stable version for your operating system.
   o Follow the installation instructions for Windows, macOS, or Linux.

o Once installed, verify the installation by opening a terminal or command prompt and running:

```bash
node -v
npm -v
```

This should display the installed versions of Node.js and npm (Node's package manager).

2. **Set Up a Code Editor:**

   o You'll need a code editor to write your Node.js applications. A popular choice is Visual Studio Code (VSCode), which offers great support for JavaScript and Node.js.

3. **Create a New Project:**

   o Open your terminal and create a new directory for your project:

```bash
mkdir my-real-time-app
cd my-real-time-app
```

   o Initialize a new Node.js project:

```bash
```

19

```
npm init -y
```

This creates a `package.json` file that will manage your project dependencies.

4. **Install Required Packages:**
   o For real-time web apps, you'll typically need WebSocket libraries. One popular library for Node.js is `socket.io`, which simplifies the process of adding real-time communication to your app.
   o Install `socket.io` by running:

```
bash
```

```
npm install socket.io
```

Introduction to JavaScript and Node.js Fundamentals

Before diving into building real-time web apps with Node.js, it's essential to understand the fundamentals of JavaScript and Node.js. Here are the key concepts to grasp:

1. **JavaScript Basics:**
   o **Variables:** In JavaScript, you declare variables using `let`, `const`, or `var`.

- **Functions:** Functions are blocks of code that can be executed when called. JavaScript supports both named and anonymous functions.
- **Events and Callbacks:** JavaScript heavily relies on events and callbacks. Functions can be passed as arguments to handle asynchronous operations, such as data fetching.
- **Objects and Arrays:** JavaScript uses objects (key-value pairs) and arrays (ordered collections) to store data.

2. **Node.js Basics:**
   - **Modules:** Node.js has a modular architecture. You can use built-in modules like `http`, `fs`, and `path` or install external libraries from npm.
   - **Event Loop:** The event loop is the core of Node.js, enabling it to handle multiple requests concurrently without blocking other operations.
   - **Streams:** Streams are used to handle data in chunks, useful for real-time data processing and large data sets.
   - **File System (fs) Module:** Node.js provides the `fs` module for interacting with the file system, allowing you to read and write files asynchronously.

This chapter provides a foundational understanding of real-time web apps, why Node.js is a great fit for them, and the basic setup needed to get started. In the following chapters, we will dive deeper into building real-world applications with Node.js, including how to handle real-time communication and manage scalability.

CHAPTER 2

UNDERSTANDING WEBSOCKETS AND REAL-TIME COMMUNICATION

What are WebSockets?

WebSockets are a protocol for full-duplex communication channels over a single, long-lived connection between the client (e.g., a web browser) and the server. This protocol allows for bidirectional communication, meaning both the client and the server can send messages to each other at any time, without waiting for the other party to initiate the communication. WebSockets are ideal for real-time web applications like online gaming, live chat, and real-time notifications.

WebSockets are an improvement over traditional HTTP because they allow continuous data exchange, eliminating the need for repeated HTTP requests and responses. Once the connection is established, it remains open, allowing for quick, low-latency communication between the client and server.

Key features of WebSockets:

- **Persistent connection:** WebSocket establishes a persistent connection that remains open, allowing for continuous communication.

- **Low latency:** Data can be transmitted in real-time with minimal delay.

- **Full-duplex communication:** Both the client and server can send messages to each other simultaneously.

- **Efficient use of resources:** Since the connection stays open, WebSockets avoid the overhead of repeatedly opening and closing connections.

Real-world Example of WebSockets: In a real-time messaging app, once a user opens the app, a WebSocket connection is established. As the user sends and receives messages, the server pushes the updates to the client instantly. No need for the user to refresh their browser or wait for new data to load—everything is updated in real-time.

How WebSockets Work in Real-Time Applications

WebSockets operate on a different communication paradigm compared to traditional HTTP. While HTTP is a request-response protocol, WebSockets work by establishing a long-lived connection that allows both parties to send messages asynchronously.

Steps to establishing a WebSocket connection:

1. **Client sends an HTTP request to the server:** The WebSocket connection is initiated with an HTTP request. This request contains an `Upgrade` header, signaling that the client wants to upgrade the connection to a WebSocket.

2. **Server accepts the connection upgrade:** The server responds with a status code (usually 101) and switches the protocol from HTTP to WebSocket.

3. **Persistent WebSocket connection:** Once the connection is established, the client and server can send messages to each other at any time. The connection remains open for as long as needed, allowing real-time, low-latency communication.

Key WebSocket Events:

- **open:** Triggered when the WebSocket connection is successfully established.
- **message:** Fired when a message is received from the other party.
- **close:** Triggered when the WebSocket connection is closed.
- **error:** Fired when an error occurs on the WebSocket connection.

Real-world Example: In a multiplayer online game, the client establishes a WebSocket connection with the game server. The game state (e.g., player positions, scores) is continuously updated in real-time and pushed to all connected clients. As players make moves or perform actions, their updates are sent to the server and broadcast to other players' clients.

The Difference Between WebSockets, HTTP, and Long-Polling

While WebSockets provide an efficient method for real-time communication, there are other methods that have been used historically. Let's compare WebSockets with HTTP and long-polling, two other common communication techniques.

1. HTTP:

- **Request-Response Model:** In HTTP, the client sends a request to the server, and the server sends a response. Each request is independent, and after the response is sent, the connection is closed.

- **No Persistent Connection:** After the client receives a response, the connection is closed, making it inefficient for real-time updates. For real-time apps, this means the client would need to repeatedly send requests to the server to fetch new data (polling).

- **Latency:** Due to the overhead of establishing new connections for each request and response, the latency is higher compared to WebSockets.

2. Long-Polling:

- **Simulating Real-Time Communication:** Long-polling is a technique where the client sends a request to the server, and the server holds the request open until new data is available. When the data is ready, the server responds to the client with the updated information.
- **Not True Real-Time:** While long-polling can simulate real-time behavior by holding the connection open, it is not as efficient as WebSockets because it still relies on sending requests to the server and waiting for responses. After receiving a response, the client immediately sends another request, causing additional overhead.
- **Latency:** Long-polling can still introduce higher latency compared to WebSockets because the server has to handle multiple open connections and repeatedly wait for new data to send to clients.

3. WebSockets:

- **Full-Duplex Communication:** WebSockets offer bidirectional communication, where both the client and server can send messages independently of each other. This is the main advantage over HTTP and long-polling.

- **Persistent Connection:** WebSocket provides a persistent, open connection, allowing real-time data transmission without the need for repetitive requests. Once the connection is established, messages can be pushed to the client as soon as they are available, reducing latency significantly.

- **Low Latency and Efficient Communication:** WebSockets are more efficient for real-time communication, as they remove the overhead of HTTP request/response cycles and eliminate the need for continuous polling.

Comparison Summary:

Feature	HTTP	Long-Polling	WebSockets
Communication model	Request-Response	Client-initiated with hold	Full-duplex (bidirectional)
Connection	Closed after each request	Connection held open	Persistent (open connection)
Latency	High	Moderate	Low

Feature	HTTP	Long-Polling	WebSockets
Efficiency	Low	Moderate	High
Real-Time Capabilities	No	Simulated	True real-time

Setting Up a WebSocket Server in Node.js

Setting up a WebSocket server in Node.js is relatively simple using libraries like ws or Socket.IO. Here's how to set up a basic WebSocket server using the ws library:

1. Install the ws library: First, install the ws package using npm:

bash

```
npm install ws
```

2. Create a WebSocket server: Create a new file, server.js, and set up a simple WebSocket server:

javascript

```
const WebSocket = require('ws');
const wss = new WebSocket.Server({ port: 8080 });

wss.on('connection', (ws) => {
```

29

```
console.log('New client connected');

// Send a welcome message to the client
ws.send('Welcome to the WebSocket server!');

// Set up a message listener from the client
ws.on('message', (message) => {
  console.log(`Received message: ${message}`);
  // Echo the message back to the client
  ws.send(`You said: ${message}`);
});

// Handle the closing of the connection
ws.on('close', () => {
  console.log('Client disconnected');
});
});
```

3. Test the WebSocket server: To test the server, you can use a WebSocket client, like the browser's JavaScript console, or create another Node.js client.

In the browser console:

```
javascript

const ws = new WebSocket('ws://localhost:8080');

ws.onopen = () => {
  console.log('Connected to WebSocket server');
```

```
  ws.send('Hello, server!');
};

ws.onmessage = (event) => {
  console.log('Received   from   server:   '   +
event.data);
};
```

4. Run the WebSocket server: Execute the `server.js` file:

```
bash

node server.js
```

You should now have a running WebSocket server on port `8080` that can send and receive messages from the client.

This chapter covered the core concepts of WebSockets and their application in real-time communication. Understanding the difference between WebSockets, HTTP, and long-polling is key to choosing the right communication protocol for your application. In the following chapters, we will explore how to incorporate WebSockets into your Node.js real-time applications, handling more complex use cases and scaling your app for large audiences.

CHAPTER 3

BUILDING YOUR FIRST REAL-TIME CHAT APPLICATION

Introduction to Chat Apps as a Real-Time Use Case

Real-time chat applications are one of the most popular use cases for WebSockets and real-time communication. Whether for personal use or business purposes, chat apps allow users to send and receive messages instantly, making them an essential part of our daily digital interactions. Real-time chat apps range from simple one-on-one messaging platforms to complex group chats, team collaboration tools, and even customer service chatbots.

Key features of chat apps that require real-time communication:

- **Instant Messaging:** Messages are sent and received immediately, without delays, providing a seamless experience for users.
- **Notifications:** Users are notified when they receive new messages, even when they are not actively using the app.
- **Group Chats and Multi-user Support:** Real-time communication is extended to groups, allowing multiple users to chat in a single session.

- **Typing Indicators and Read Receipts:** Real-time updates, such as showing when a user is typing or when a message has been read, are essential to creating an interactive chat experience.

Building a real-time chat app is a great way to understand the practical applications of WebSockets, as it involves continuous communication between the client (user) and the server, ensuring fast, responsive interactions.

Implementing WebSocket for Real-Time Messaging

To build a real-time chat app, the most effective method is using WebSockets. WebSockets allow you to establish a persistent connection between the client and server, which is crucial for sending and receiving messages instantaneously.

In this section, we'll break down how to implement WebSockets for real-time messaging:

1. **Setting Up the WebSocket Server:**
   o As discussed in Chapter 2, WebSocket servers allow bidirectional communication between the server and client. Using Node.js, you can set up a WebSocket server with the `ws` library.

33

Installing the necessary package: First, install the `ws` package:

```bash
npm install ws
```

Setting up the WebSocket server: Create a `chatServer.js` file to handle the WebSocket connection.

```javascript
const WebSocket = require('ws');
const wss = new WebSocket.Server({ port: 8080 });

wss.on('connection', (ws) => {
  console.log('New client connected');

  // Send a message to the client when they connect
  ws.send('Welcome to the chat app!');

  // Handle incoming messages
  ws.on('message', (message) => {
    console.log(`Received message: ${message}`);
```

```
    // Broadcast the message to all
connected clients
    wss.clients.forEach(client => {
        if (client !== ws &&
client.readyState === WebSocket.OPEN) {
            client.send(message);
        }
    });
  });

  // Handle client disconnection
  ws.on('close', () => {
    console.log('Client disconnected');
  });
});
```

- o In this WebSocket server setup:
  - When a new client connects, a welcome message is sent to them.
  - Any message sent from one client is broadcasted to all other connected clients.
  - When a client disconnects, the server logs the disconnection.

2. **Client-Side WebSocket Implementation:** On the client side, you need to connect to the WebSocket server and send/receive messages.

Creating a simple HTML and JavaScript chat client:

Create a file chatClient.html for the front-end user interface:

html

```html
<!DOCTYPE html>
<html lang="en">
<head>
  <meta charset="UTF-8">
  <meta                     name="viewport"
content="width=device-width,        initial-
scale=1.0">
  <title>Real-Time Chat App</title>
  <style>
    #chat { width: 300px;  height:  400px;
overflow-y: scroll; border: 1px solid #ccc;
padding: 10px; }
    #message { width: 240px; }
  </style>
</head>
<body>
  <h2>Real-Time Chat App</h2>
  <div id="chat"></div>
  <input     type="text"      id="message"
placeholder="Type a message..." />
  <button
onclick="sendMessage()">Send</button>
```

```
<script>
  const          ws          =          new
WebSocket('ws://localhost:8080');

  // Display incoming messages
  ws.onmessage = (event) => {
    const            chat            =
document.getElementById('chat');
    chat.innerHTML                    +=
`<p>${event.data}</p>`;
    chat.scrollTop = chat.scrollHeight;
  };

  // Send message function
  function sendMessage() {
    const          messageInput          =
document.getElementById('message');
    const message = messageInput.value;
    if (message) {
      ws.send(message);   //  Send  the
message to the server
      messageInput.value = ''; // Clear
the input field
    }
  }
</script>
</body>
</html>
```

o   In this simple client:

- When a message is sent, it is transmitted to the WebSocket server.
- Incoming messages are displayed in the chat area, and the chat automatically scrolls down to show the most recent messages.

Basic Chat App Architecture

Now that you've learned how to set up WebSocket communication, let's look at the basic architecture of a real-time chat app.

1. **Client-Side:**
   o The client-side consists of the user interface, which includes the chat area (where messages are displayed) and an input field (where users can type messages).
   o The client establishes a WebSocket connection to the server and listens for incoming messages.
   o When a user sends a message, it is transmitted through the WebSocket to the server, which then broadcasts it to other connected clients.
2. **Server-Side:**
   o The server manages all WebSocket connections and handles the broadcasting of messages.

- o The server listens for incoming connections from clients and keeps track of all active WebSocket connections.
- o When a message is received, the server pushes it to all connected clients (except the sender).

High-Level Architecture:

- **WebSocket Server:** A Node.js server running the WebSocket protocol.
- **WebSocket Clients:** Web browsers or devices that connect to the server and exchange messages in real-time.
- **Communication Flow:**
  - o Client A sends a message → WebSocket Server receives the message → Server broadcasts the message to all other connected clients (including Client B).

Real-World Example: Creating a Simple Chat App with Node.js

Let's walk through the process of creating a simple real-time chat application using Node.js and WebSockets.

1. **Step 1: Setting Up the WebSocket Server:**
   - o As shown earlier, install `ws` and create a WebSocket server in `chatServer.js` that

39

listens on port 8080 and broadcasts messages to all connected clients.

2. **Step 2: Building the Front-End:**
   o Create a basic HTML page for the client-side chat interface. The client connects to the WebSocket server and allows users to send and receive messages.

3. **Step 3: Testing the Chat App:**
   o Start the WebSocket server:

```bash
node chatServer.js
```

   o Open `chatClient.html` in multiple browser tabs and test the chat app. Messages typed in one tab should appear in all the other tabs in real-time.

Conclusion

In this chapter, you've learned how to build a simple real-time chat application using WebSockets in Node.js. We explored how WebSockets enable low-latency, bidirectional communication between clients and servers, and how this makes them ideal for building real-time messaging apps. You've also seen how to set up a WebSocket server, implement the client-side chat interface, and manage message broadcasting.

In the following chapters, we will dive deeper into enhancing this basic chat app with more features like user authentication, handling different rooms or channels, and scaling your application for a large number of users.

CHAPTER 4

NODE.JS EVENT LOOP AND ASYNCHRONOUS PROGRAMMING

Understanding Node.js's Single-Threaded Event Loop

One of the key features that sets Node.js apart from traditional server-side environments is its **single-threaded event loop**. While most web servers create a new thread for each incoming request, Node.js uses a more efficient, non-blocking, and event-driven approach to handle multiple requests simultaneously with a single thread.

What is the Event Loop?

- The **event loop** in Node.js is a mechanism that continuously checks if there are any tasks to be executed. It is responsible for handling asynchronous operations, such as I/O (Input/Output) operations (e.g., reading files, accessing databases, handling network requests) without blocking the execution of other operations.

- This allows Node.js to handle many concurrent connections with minimal resources.

Here's how the event loop works:

1. **Incoming Request:** When a request is made to a Node.js application (e.g., an HTTP request), it is passed to the event loop.
2. **Task Queues:** The event loop checks the task queues for any tasks (callbacks or promises) that need to be executed.
3. **Executing the Task:** If the task is synchronous, the event loop executes it immediately. If it is asynchronous, the event loop delegates the task to a worker (e.g., reading from a file, querying a database), and once the task completes, the callback is placed in the task queue.
4. **Non-blocking:** During I/O operations, the event loop is free to continue processing other tasks, ensuring that the application remains responsive.

Because Node.js is single-threaded, it doesn't need to create a new thread for every incoming request, which makes it lightweight and fast for I/O-bound tasks. This characteristic is essential for real-time applications that require handling many simultaneous connections, such as chat apps or live updates.

Real-World Example of Node.js Event Loop: Imagine a real-time chat application with thousands of active users. When a user sends a message, the message is passed through the event loop and processed asynchronously. This means while one message is being written to a database or broadcasted to other users, the event loop can continue to handle other incoming messages without waiting for the current task to finish. This approach ensures high performance and responsiveness.

The Importance of Asynchronous Programming in Real-Time Apps

Asynchronous programming is crucial for building efficient and scalable real-time applications. Since real-time apps often handle many concurrent connections and perform tasks like querying a database, making HTTP requests, or reading files, traditional synchronous programming would be too slow and inefficient.

Why Asynchronous Programming Matters:

1. **Non-blocking Operations:** With asynchronous programming, tasks such as file reads, database queries, or API calls do not block the main thread. Instead, they are offloaded to the background, allowing the event loop to continue processing other tasks.

2. **Scalability:** Asynchronous programming helps Node.js scale efficiently, enabling it to handle thousands of concurrent connections. This is essential for real-time

apps like messaging platforms, where many users interact with the system simultaneously.

3. **Improved Performance:** Non-blocking I/O operations allow Node.js to execute tasks in parallel, which leads to faster response times and greater throughput, particularly for I/O-bound tasks.

Real-World Example: Consider a real-time stock trading app. When a user buys a stock, the app needs to check the stock price, verify the transaction with a bank, and update the user's portfolio. Each of these tasks could involve time-consuming network requests or database queries. In a synchronous environment, each request would block the next task until it completes. However, by using asynchronous programming in Node.js, the system can continue responding to other users' requests while waiting for these tasks to complete.

Callbacks, Promises, and Async/Await in Node.js

Node.js relies heavily on asynchronous programming patterns to handle I/O tasks, and there are different approaches to managing asynchronous operations in JavaScript. The three most common methods are **callbacks**, **promises**, and **async/await**.

Callbacks

A **callback** is a function that is passed as an argument to another function and is executed when that function completes. In Node.js, many built-in APIs, such as file reading or HTTP requests, use callbacks to handle asynchronous tasks.

Example of a callback:

javascript

```
const fs = require('fs');

// Asynchronous file reading with a callback
fs.readFile('example.txt', 'utf8', (err, data)
=> {
  if (err) {
    console.error('Error reading file:', err);
  } else {
    console.log('File content:', data);
  }
});
```

In this example:

- The `fs.readFile()` function reads the contents of a file asynchronously.

- The callback function is executed once the file reading operation is completed, either with an error or with the file data.

However, callbacks can lead to "callback hell" or "pyramid of doom," especially when there are multiple nested asynchronous tasks, making the code harder to read and maintain.

Promises

A **promise** is an object that represents the eventual completion (or failure) of an asynchronous operation and its resulting value. Promises provide a cleaner way to handle asynchronous operations compared to callbacks.

A promise can be in one of three states:

- **Pending:** The initial state, before the operation is completed.
- **Resolved (Fulfilled):** The operation was completed successfully.
- **Rejected:** The operation failed.

Example of a promise:

javascript

```javascript
const fs = require('fs').promises;
```

```
// Using promises to read a file
fs.readFile('example.txt', 'utf8')
  .then((data) => {
    console.log('File content:', data);
  })
  .catch((err) => {
    console.error('Error reading file:', err);
  });
```

In this example:

- `fs.readFile()` returns a promise that resolves with the file content.
- `.then()` handles the success case, while `.catch()` handles errors.

Promises allow you to chain multiple asynchronous operations, making the code more readable and easier to manage than using nested callbacks.

Async/Await

Async/await is a more modern and clean approach to working with promises. The `async` keyword is used to define an asynchronous function, and `await` is used to pause the execution of the function until a promise is resolved.

Example of async/await:

48

```javascript

const fs = require('fs').promises;

async function readFile() {
  try {
    const          data          =          await
fs.readFile('example.txt', 'utf8');
    console.log('File content:', data);
  } catch (err) {
    console.error('Error reading file:', err);
  }
}

readFile();
```

In this example:

- The readFile() function is marked as async.
- The await keyword is used to pause execution until the fs.readFile() promise is resolved.
- This approach makes asynchronous code look more like synchronous code, which improves readability and reduces the risk of errors.

Real-World Example: Managing Asynchronous Events in a Node.js App

Let's build a simple example to demonstrate how Node.js manages asynchronous operations. We'll simulate a real-time app where users can submit requests that involve asynchronous tasks like reading data from a database, processing it, and sending back a response.

1. **Simulating Database Access:** Assume that the app needs to read user data from a database, process it, and return the result to the client.
2. **Using Async/Await to Manage the Asynchronous Flow:**

javascript

```javascript
const fetchUserData = (userId) => {
  // Simulate database access with a delay
  return new Promise((resolve, reject) => {
    setTimeout(() => {
      const userData = { id: userId, name: 'John
Doe' };
      resolve(userData);
    }, 1000); // Simulate delay of 1 second
  });
};
```

```
const processUserData = async (userId) => {
  try {
    const user = await fetchUserData(userId);
    console.log('User Data:', user);
    // Process the data (e.g., apply business
logic)
    return `Processed data for user:
${user.name}`;
  } catch (err) {
    console.error('Error fetching user data:',
err);
  }
};


processUserData(1).then((result) => {
  console.log(result); // Output: Processed data
for user: John Doe
});
```

In this example:

- The `fetchUserData()` function simulates a database query that returns user data after a delay.
- The `processUserData()` function is `async` and uses `await` to handle the asynchronous database query and process the data sequentially.

By using async/await, the flow of asynchronous code is much clearer and easier to follow than if we used callbacks or promises alone.

Conclusion

In this chapter, we explored the importance of Node.js's single-threaded event loop and how it enables efficient asynchronous programming. We learned how asynchronous programming is crucial for building scalable real-time applications and how callbacks, promises, and async/await are the primary tools for handling asynchronous operations in Node.js.

By leveraging these techniques, Node.js can manage I/O-bound tasks efficiently, enabling real-time applications to handle many concurrent users without blocking the main thread. In the next chapters, we will explore how to use these asynchronous programming techniques to build and scale real-time applications, such as chat apps and live data feeds.

CHAPTER 5

EXPRESS.JS FOR BUILDING APIS

Introduction to Express.js for Creating APIs

Express.js is a minimal and flexible web application framework for Node.js that simplifies the process of building robust APIs. It provides a set of powerful tools for handling HTTP requests, middleware, and routing, making it an ideal choice for building both traditional web apps and real-time applications.

For real-time applications, APIs serve as the communication backbone between the client (user) and the server. Express.js enables you to build APIs that handle different types of requests (such as retrieving data or sending data to the server) with minimal code.

Key Features of Express.js:

- **Routing:** Express makes it easy to define routes that handle various HTTP methods (GET, POST, PUT, DELETE).
- **Middleware:** Express uses middleware functions to modify requests and responses before they reach the route

handler. This allows for powerful pre-processing, authentication, logging, etc.

- **Handling Requests and Responses:** Express provides convenient methods for sending HTTP responses and handling incoming requests.

Express.js abstracts away the complexities of setting up and configuring a Node.js server, making it easier to focus on building the application's logic. It is the most popular framework in the Node.js ecosystem and is widely used for building RESTful APIs and other types of server-side applications.

Building RESTful APIs for Real-Time Apps

A **RESTful API** (Representational State Transfer) is an architectural style for designing networked applications. It relies on stateless communication and uses standard HTTP methods such as GET, POST, PUT, and DELETE. RESTful APIs are the most common type of API used for web applications because they are lightweight, flexible, and easy to maintain.

For real-time apps, RESTful APIs allow clients to interact with the server to fetch, submit, and update data. While WebSockets are used for continuous communication, REST APIs are commonly used for handling operations like user authentication, data retrieval, and other CRUD (Create, Read, Update, Delete) operations.

Building a RESTful API with Express.js involves the following steps:

1. **Defining Routes:** Use Express to define routes that handle HTTP requests (GET, POST, PUT, DELETE).
2. **Handling Requests:** For each route, specify the logic to handle incoming requests and generate the appropriate response.
3. **Sending Responses:** Use Express's response object to send data (usually in JSON format) back to the client.

For real-time applications, REST APIs can be used for:

- **User Authentication:** APIs for logging in, registering, and managing users.
- **Data Management:** APIs for adding, updating, and retrieving data from the database.
- **Notifications:** While real-time notifications are often handled via WebSockets, REST APIs can be used to fetch notifications or mark them as read.

Handling HTTP Requests and Responses

Express.js simplifies the process of handling HTTP requests and responses. Let's break down how HTTP requests and responses work in an Express application:

1. **Handling HTTP Requests:**
   o When a client sends a request (e.g., a browser or another server), it contains various information such as the HTTP method (GET, POST, etc.), headers, and request body.
   o In Express, you define **routes** to handle these requests. A route consists of the URL path and the HTTP method.
2. **Responding to Requests:**
   o Once the request is processed, Express provides a way to send a response. You can send different types of responses, such as status codes, HTML, or JSON data.
3. **Common HTTP Methods:**
   o **GET:** Retrieve data from the server.
   o **POST:** Submit data to the server (e.g., creating a new user).
   o **PUT:** Update existing data on the server.
   o **DELETE:** Remove data from the server.

Example of defining a route to handle HTTP requests:

```javascript
const express = require('express');
const app = express();

// Middleware to parse incoming JSON requests
app.use(express.json());

// GET route - Retrieve data
app.get('/users', (req, res) => {
  // Fetch users from the database (simulated
with an array)
  const users = [{ id: 1, name: 'John Doe' }, {
id: 2, name: 'Jane Smith' }];
  res.json(users); // Send response as JSON
});

// POST route - Create a new user
app.post('/users', (req, res) => {
  const newUser = req.body;
  // Logic to save the user to the database
(simulated)
  newUser.id = 3; // Assign a new ID
  res.status(201).json(newUser);      //      Send
response with a 201 status code
});

// PUT route - Update an existing user
app.put('/users/:id', (req, res) => {
```

```javascript
  const userId = req.params.id;
  const updatedUser = req.body;
  // Logic to update the user in the database
(simulated)
  updatedUser.id = userId; // Update user ID
  res.json(updatedUser); // Send updated user
data
});


// DELETE route - Delete a user
app.delete('/users/:id', (req, res) => {
  const userId = req.params.id;
  // Logic to delete the user from the database
(simulated)
  res.status(204).send(); // No content to
return, so status code 204
});


// Start the server
app.listen(3000, () => {
  console.log('Server          running          on
http://localhost:3000');
});
```

In this example:

- **GET /users**: Fetches a list of users.
- **POST /users**: Creates a new user by sending data in the request body.

- **PUT /users/:id**: Updates an existing user by providing their ID in the URL and updated data in the request body.
- **DELETE /users/:id**: Deletes a user by their ID.

Each of these routes handles the HTTP request, processes the data, and sends an appropriate response back to the client. In a real-time app, these APIs could be used for tasks like user management, data fetching, and updating.

Real-World Example: API Design for a Real-Time Application

Let's now create a real-world example of an API design for a simple real-time notification system. In this scenario, users will receive notifications about different events, and the API will handle the creation, retrieval, and marking of notifications as read.

1. **Defining Routes for the Notification System:**
   - **POST /notifications**: To create a new notification.
   - **GET /notifications**: To retrieve a list of notifications.
   - **PUT /notifications/:id**: To mark a notification as read.
2. **Setting Up the API with Express:**

```javascript
```

```
const express = require('express');
const app = express();
app.use(express.json());

let notifications = [
  { id: 1, message: 'New message from John',
read: false },
  { id: 2, message: 'Your order has been
shipped', read: false },
];

// POST route - Create a new notification
app.post('/notifications', (req, res) => {
  const { message } = req.body;
  const newNotification = { id:
notifications.length + 1, message, read: false };
  notifications.push(newNotification);
  res.status(201).json(newNotification);       //
Return the created notification
});

// GET route - Retrieve all notifications
app.get('/notifications', (req, res) => {
  res.json(notifications); // Return the list of
notifications
});

// PUT route - Mark a notification as read
app.put('/notifications/:id', (req, res) => {
```

```
const              notificationId           =
parseInt(req.params.id);
  const notification = notifications.find(n =>
n.id === notificationId);
  if (notification) {
   notification.read = true;
    res.json(notification);    //    Return    the
updated notification
  } else {
    res.status(404).json({              message:
'Notification not found' });
  }
});

// Start the server
app.listen(3000, () => {
  console.log('Notification    API    running    on
http://localhost:3000');
});
```

In this example:

- **POST /notifications** creates a new notification with a message.
- **GET /notifications** retrieves a list of all notifications.
- **PUT /notifications/:id** marks a specific notification as read by its ID.

Real-World Use Case for the API: Imagine this API as part of a real-time messaging or e-commerce platform. Users can be notified in real-time when they receive new messages or when their orders are processed. The real-time part would typically be handled by WebSockets for live notifications, while RESTful APIs like the one above would manage the creation, retrieval, and updating of notifications.

Conclusion

In this chapter, we introduced **Express.js**, a powerful framework for building APIs in Node.js. We explored how to create RESTful APIs, handle HTTP requests and responses, and manage routes. We also walked through a real-world example of designing an API for a real-time notification system, demonstrating how Express.js can be used to handle real-time app functionalities like user notifications.

In the next chapters, we will continue to expand on building real-time features in Node.js and integrate these APIs with WebSockets to achieve full-duplex communication for applications such as chat apps, live updates, and more.

CHAPTER 6

REAL-TIME DATA WITH REDIS

Why Redis is Useful for Real-Time Data Management

Redis is an open-source, in-memory data store widely used as a database, cache, and message broker. It is designed to handle high-throughput and low-latency operations, making it an ideal choice for managing real-time data. For real-time applications such as messaging platforms, live feeds, and collaborative tools, Redis excels in managing and sharing data between distributed systems in an efficient manner.

Key Advantages of Redis for Real-Time Data:

- **In-Memory Storage:** Redis stores data in memory, offering extremely fast read and write operations compared to traditional disk-based databases. This speed is crucial for real-time applications where every millisecond counts.

- **Atomic Operations:** Redis supports atomic operations on its data structures, ensuring consistency even in highly concurrent environments.

- **Persistence:** While Redis primarily operates as an in-memory data store, it can be configured for persistence (via snapshots or logs) to avoid data loss during restarts.

- **Data Structures:** Redis supports a variety of data types such as strings, hashes, lists, sets, and sorted sets. These structures are optimized for different use cases, allowing developers to choose the most appropriate one for the data they are managing.

- **Pub/Sub (Publish/Subscribe) Messaging System:** Redis can act as a powerful messaging system, making it easy to implement real-time communication between different components of an application. This is particularly useful in event-driven systems and chat applications.

Redis's **Publish/Subscribe (pub/sub)** messaging model is particularly beneficial for real-time applications where messages need to be broadcasted to multiple subscribers instantly. By using Redis as a pub/sub broker, you can decouple components of your system and allow them to communicate asynchronously.

Using Redis as a Pub/Sub Messaging System

In a **pub/sub** system, a **publisher** sends messages to a **channel**, while **subscribers** listen to specific channels for new messages. When a message is published to a channel, all subscribers to that channel receive the message immediately. This model is highly efficient for real-time applications like chat rooms, live sports feeds, and news updates.

How Redis Pub/Sub Works:

1. **Publisher:** A client (or service) publishes messages to a specific channel in Redis.
2. **Subscriber:** One or more clients subscribe to a specific channel to receive messages published to it.
3. **Message Delivery:** When a message is published to a channel, all subscribers to that channel instantly receive the message.

The beauty of Redis's pub/sub model is that it provides a lightweight, scalable, and low-latency way to broadcast real-time updates to multiple clients without the need for direct communication between each publisher and subscriber.

Redis Pub/Sub Commands:

- **PUBLISH channel message:** The publisher sends a message to the specified channel.
- **SUBSCRIBE channel:** A client subscribes to a specific channel and starts receiving messages sent to that channel.
- **UNSUBSCRIBE channel:** A client stops receiving messages from the channel.

Redis Pub/Sub is ideal for scenarios where multiple clients need to receive the same message simultaneously, such as real-time notifications or updates to a live feed.

Setting Up Redis with Node.js

To integrate Redis with your Node.js application, you'll need the `redis` client for Node.js. This package provides methods to interact with Redis, including support for pub/sub messaging.

Here's how to set up Redis with Node.js:

1. **Install Redis:** If you don't already have Redis installed, download and install it from the official website: https://redis.io/download.

2. **Install Redis Client for Node.js:** Use npm to install the Redis client package:

```bash
bash
```

```bash
npm install redis
```

3. **Create a Redis Client in Node.js:** The Redis client allows your Node.js application to connect to the Redis server and interact with it.

   Example of setting up a Redis client:

```javascript

const redis = require('redis');

// Create a Redis client
const client = redis.createClient();

client.on('connect', () => {
  console.log('Connected to Redis...');
});

client.on('error', (err) => {
  console.error('Redis error: ' + err);
});
```

4. **Using Pub/Sub with Redis in Node.js:** You can use the `redis` client to subscribe to channels and publish messages.

   Example of a basic pub/sub implementation:

```javascript

const redis = require('redis');
const subscriber = redis.createClient();
const publisher = redis.createClient();

// Subscriber listens to a channel
subscriber.subscribe('chat_room');
```

```
subscriber.on('message',          (channel,
message) => {
  console.log(`Received          message:
${message} on channel: ${channel}`);
});

// Publisher sends messages to the channel
setInterval(() => {
  const message = `New message at ${new
Date().toISOString()}`;
  publisher.publish('chat_room', message);
}, 3000); // Every 3 seconds
```

In this example:

- The **subscriber** listens to the chat_room channel and logs any messages it receives.
- The **publisher** sends a new message to the chat_room channel every 3 seconds.
- Every subscriber connected to the chat_room channel will instantly receive the new messages.

Real-World Example: Using Redis to Manage Chat Room Data

Now, let's look at a real-world example of using Redis with Node.js to manage chat room data. In a chat application, we might want to store and broadcast messages in real-time while keeping track of different chat rooms.

Steps to Build the Chat Room Application:

1. **Publisher:** When a user sends a message in a chat room, the server publishes the message to Redis.

2. **Subscriber:** All clients that are connected to that chat room subscribe to the relevant Redis channel and receive the new messages instantly.

3. **Storing Message History:** Redis can also be used to store message history for a particular chat room, allowing clients to retrieve previous messages when they join the room.

Setting Up the Chat Room with Redis:

javascript

```javascript
const express = require('express');
const redis = require('redis');

const app = express();
const publisher = redis.createClient();
const subscriber = redis.createClient();

// Chat room data
const chatRooms = {};
```

```javascript
// Subscribe to chat room channels
subscriber.on('message', (channel, message) => {
  console.log(`Received message in ${channel}:
${message}`);
  if (!chatRooms[channel]) {
    chatRooms[channel] = [];
  }
  chatRooms[channel].push(message);
});


// Listen to messages for chat room 'general'
subscriber.subscribe('general');

// HTTP endpoint to send a message to the chat
room
app.post('/sendMessage/:room', (req, res) => {
  const { room } = req.params;
  const { message } = req.query;

  // Publish message to Redis
  publisher.publish(room, message);
  res.status(200).send('Message sent!');
});

// HTTP endpoint to get the message history of a
chat room
app.get('/history/:room', (req, res) => {
  const { room } = req.params;
  const history = chatRooms[room] || [];
```

```
    res.json({ history });
});

// Start the server
app.listen(3000, () => {
    console.log('Server          running          on
http://localhost:3000');
});
```

In this example:

- The **publisher** sends messages to a specific chat room using Redis.
- The **subscriber** listens to messages from the `general` chat room and stores them in an in-memory object (`chatRooms`) that represents the history of each room.
- The `/sendMessage/:room` endpoint allows clients to send messages to a specified room.
- The `/history/:room` endpoint retrieves the message history for a chat room.

How It Works:

- When a user sends a message, it is published to the Redis channel corresponding to the chat room.
- All subscribers to that channel (clients in the room) will receive the message and can process it (e.g., display it in their UI).

- Clients can request the message history for a specific chat room, and Redis can store this history if configured for persistence.

Conclusion

In this chapter, we explored how Redis can be used for real-time data management, focusing on its capabilities as a pub/sub messaging system. We saw how Redis enables efficient real-time communication by broadcasting messages to multiple subscribers simultaneously. Additionally, we learned how to set up Redis with Node.js and created a simple real-time chat room application that utilizes Redis to publish and subscribe to messages.

Redis is a powerful tool for building scalable and responsive real-time applications, and in the next chapters, we will continue to explore how to integrate Redis with other components of a real-time web application.

CHAPTER 7

HANDLING AUTHENTICATION AND USER MANAGEMENT

Introduction to Authentication in Real-Time Applications

Authentication is a critical aspect of any web application, including real-time applications. It ensures that users are who they say they are and that they can only access resources they are authorized to use. In real-time apps, where users are constantly interacting with the system (such as in messaging platforms, live updates, or collaboration tools), authentication plays an even more important role in maintaining security and providing personalized experiences.

In real-time applications, the challenge of authentication involves not only verifying the identity of users but also ensuring that the authentication process does not interfere with the seamless, low-latency experience that real-time apps provide. This requires using modern and efficient authentication methods that work well with the stateless nature of real-time communication protocols like WebSockets.

Common types of authentication in web applications include:

- **Session-based Authentication:** Storing session data on the server and linking it to a session ID stored in the user's browser.

- **Token-based Authentication:** Issuing tokens (such as JWT) to the user upon successful login, which are used to authenticate subsequent requests.

In real-time apps, **stateless** authentication (such as token-based authentication) is often preferred because it does not require the server to keep track of active sessions, making it more scalable.

Implementing JWT (JSON Web Tokens) for Authentication

JSON Web Tokens (JWT) are a popular way to authenticate users in modern web applications, particularly for APIs and real-time apps. JWT allows for a stateless, scalable, and secure method of transmitting user authentication information.

A **JWT** consists of three parts:

1. **Header:** Contains information about how the token is signed (e.g., the signing algorithm).

2. **Payload:** Contains the actual data or claims, such as user information (user ID, role, etc.).

3. **Signature:** Used to verify that the token was not tampered with and that it was issued by a trusted source.

Why JWT is Ideal for Real-Time Apps:

- **Stateless Authentication:** Since JWT contains all necessary information within the token, there is no need to store session data on the server. This is particularly useful for scaling real-time apps, where the server needs to handle many concurrent users.
- **Security:** JWT is signed using a secret or a public/private key pair, ensuring the token's integrity.
- **Ease of Use:** Once the JWT is issued, it can be sent with every request, making it easy to authenticate users in real-time applications (e.g., WebSocket connections).

How JWT Works:

1. The user logs in by providing their credentials (username/password).
2. If the credentials are valid, the server generates a JWT, which contains the user's ID and any other necessary claims (e.g., roles, permissions).
3. The server sends the JWT to the client, where it is stored (commonly in localStorage or a cookie).
4. The client sends the JWT in the `Authorization` header for every subsequent request.
5. The server verifies the JWT and grants access to the requested resource if the token is valid.

Installing JWT in Node.js: To implement JWT in a Node.js app, you need the `jsonwebtoken` package.

Install the `jsonwebtoken` package using npm:

```bash
bash
```

```bash
npm install jsonwebtoken
```

Example of generating and verifying a JWT:

1. **Generating a JWT upon login:**

```javascript
javascript
```

```javascript
const jwt = require('jsonwebtoken');

// Simulate user login
const user = { id: 1, username: 'john_doe' };

// Generate a JWT
const token = jwt.sign(user, 'your-secret-key', { expiresIn: '1h' });
console.log('Generated JWT:', token);
```

2. **Verifying the JWT on each request:**

```javascript
javascript
```

```
const verifyToken = (token) => {
  try {
    const   decoded   =   jwt.verify(token,
'your-secret-key');
    console.log('Decoded JWT:', decoded);
    return decoded;
  } catch (err) {
    console.error('Invalid token:', err);
    return null;
  }
};


// Example of using the function to verify
a token
const decodedUser = verifyToken(token);
```

Managing User Sessions and Authentication in Node.js

Managing user authentication in a Node.js real-time app typically involves verifying the user's identity, issuing a JWT, and ensuring that the user has the appropriate access rights for various operations.

The typical flow for managing user sessions in a real-time app involves:

1. **User Login:** The user submits their credentials (e.g., username and password).

2. **Token Generation:** If the credentials are valid, the server generates a JWT and sends it back to the client.

3. **Token Storage:** The client stores the JWT (typically in `localStorage` or an HTTP-only cookie).

4. **Token Verification:** For each subsequent request, the client includes the JWT in the request headers (typically under `Authorization: Bearer <token>`). The server verifies the token on each request to ensure the user is authenticated.

Example: Authenticating a WebSocket Connection Using JWT WebSocket connections are typically initiated before user authentication. To authenticate WebSocket clients, you can use the JWT passed during the WebSocket handshake.

1. **Server-Side WebSocket Authentication:** In this example, the client sends the JWT in the WebSocket query string. The server verifies the token during the WebSocket connection process.

```javascript
const WebSocket = require('ws');
const jwt = require('jsonwebtoken');

const wss = new WebSocket.Server({ port: 8080 });
```

```javascript
wss.on('connection', (ws, req) => {
  const token = req.url.split('=')[1]; //
Extract token from query string

  // Verify the JWT
  jwt.verify(token,        'your-secret-key',
(err, decoded) => {
    if (err) {
      ws.send('Authentication failed');
      ws.close();
    } else {
      ws.send(`Welcome
${decoded.username}!`);
    }
  });
});
```

2. **Client-Side:** The client sends the JWT when connecting to the WebSocket server:

javascript

```javascript
const token = localStorage.getItem('jwt');
const          ws          =          new
WebSocket(`ws://localhost:8080?token=${to
ken}`);

ws.onopen = () => {
  console.log('WebSocket          connection
established');
```

```
};

ws.onmessage = (event) => {
  console.log('Received          message:',
event.data);
};
```

Real-World Example: Building Secure User Authentication in a Real-Time App

Let's build a simple real-time chat application that requires user authentication. We will implement JWT-based authentication and secure the WebSocket connection using JWT for user identity verification.

1. User Login and Token Generation:

javascript

```
const express = require('express');
const jwt = require('jsonwebtoken');
const app = express();
const bcrypt = require('bcryptjs');
const bodyParser = require('body-parser');

app.use(bodyParser.json());

// Simulated user database
```

```javascript
const users = [
  { id: 1, username: 'john_doe', password:
'$2a$10$...' } // bcrypt-hashed password
];

// Login route: Generate JWT
app.post('/login', (req, res) => {
  const { username, password } = req.body;

  const user = users.find(u => u.username ===
username);

  if (!user) {
    return    res.status(400).send('User    not
found');
  }

  // Compare password (hashed)
  bcrypt.compare(password, user.password, (err,
isMatch) => {
    if (err || !isMatch) {
      return    res.status(400).send('Invalid
password');
    }

    // Generate JWT
    const token = jwt.sign({ id: user.id,
username: user.username }, 'your-secret-key', {
expiresIn: '1h' });
```

```
    res.json({ token });
  });
});


// Start Express server
app.listen(3000,  ()  =>  console.log('Server
running on http://localhost:3000'));
```

2. WebSocket Connection with JWT Authentication:

Once the user logs in, they receive a JWT. When they connect to the WebSocket server, the server authenticates the JWT and allows the user to join the chat.

```
javascript


const WebSocket = require('ws');
const jwt = require('jsonwebtoken');


const wss = new WebSocket.Server({ port: 8080 });


wss.on('connection', (ws, req) => {
  const token = req.url.split('=')[1]; // Extract
token from URL query


  jwt.verify(token,  'your-secret-key',  (err,
decoded) => {
    if (err) {
      ws.send('Authentication failed');
      ws.close();
```

```
    } else {
      ws.send(`Welcome ${decoded.username}!`);
      // Add user to chat room (simulated)
      ws.on('message', (message) => {
        console.log(`${decoded.username}:
${message}`);
      });
    }
  });
});
```

In this example:

- **User Login:** The user logs in with their username and password, and the server generates a JWT.
- **WebSocket Authentication:** When the client connects to the WebSocket server, the JWT is sent as part of the connection request. The server verifies the JWT before allowing access.

Conclusion

In this chapter, we explored how to implement user authentication in real-time applications using JWT. We saw how to use JWT for stateless authentication and how it can be used to secure WebSocket connections. We also covered managing user sessions and authentication in Node.js, ensuring that real-time apps remain secure while providing a seamless user experience.

With JWT, you can easily scale real-time applications by decoupling authentication from the server's session management, allowing each user to authenticate and access resources independently. In the next chapters, we will continue to build on this foundation and integrate more advanced features into our real-time applications.

CHAPTER 8

SCALING REAL-TIME WEB APPS WITH NODE.JS

How to Scale Real-Time Applications

Scaling real-time applications is crucial as your app grows and starts to handle more users, requests, and data. Real-time apps, such as chat apps, live updates, or collaborative tools, often face unique scaling challenges due to the need for low-latency, high-throughput communication across multiple users.

Challenges in Scaling Real-Time Applications:

- **Concurrency:** Real-time apps need to manage many concurrent users and ensure that each user receives real-time updates without delays.
- **State Management:** For real-time apps, managing user state (e.g., session data, message history) becomes more complex as you scale.
- **Network Latency:** Maintaining fast communication between clients and servers is critical, and network latency can be an issue when dealing with a large number of clients.

To overcome these challenges, Node.js offers efficient solutions due to its non-blocking, event-driven architecture. However, scaling a Node.js application effectively requires addressing the need for horizontal scaling, load balancing, and state management.

Horizontal vs. Vertical Scaling

When scaling applications, two main strategies are often considered: **vertical scaling** and **horizontal scaling**. Let's look at how each approach applies to real-time web apps built with Node.js.

1. **Vertical Scaling (Scaling Up):**
   o Vertical scaling involves increasing the resources (CPU, RAM) of a single server to handle more users or requests. This can be done by upgrading the server hardware or moving to a larger instance in a cloud environment.
   o **Limitations:**
      ▪ You're limited by the capacity of a single server.
      ▪ While vertical scaling can improve performance in the short term, it may not be sustainable when handling large

traffic spikes or a high number of concurrent users.

2. **Horizontal Scaling (Scaling Out):**

   o Horizontal scaling involves adding more servers or instances to distribute the load, allowing the application to handle more users and requests concurrently. In the context of Node.js, this often means running multiple instances of your app on different servers or containers and using a load balancer to distribute traffic.

   o **Advantages:**

      ▪ **Improved fault tolerance:** If one server goes down, others can continue to serve requests.

      ▪ **Better load distribution:** More servers mean that the system can handle a higher number of concurrent connections, which is critical for real-time applications.

In a real-time app context, horizontal scaling is usually the preferred method, as it allows you to handle many users simultaneously without overwhelming a single server.

Load Balancing in Node.js Apps

Load balancing is a technique used to distribute incoming network traffic across multiple servers or instances, ensuring no single server gets overwhelmed. This is especially important for real-time applications, where the number of concurrent users can fluctuate frequently.

How Load Balancing Works:

- When a client sends a request, the load balancer determines which server (or instance) should handle the request and forwards it accordingly.
- The load balancer monitors the health of the servers to ensure that only healthy servers are used for handling requests.

Popular Load Balancing Techniques:

1. **Round-robin:** Requests are distributed evenly across all available servers in a circular manner.
2. **Least connections:** The load balancer sends the request to the server with the least number of active connections.
3. **IP hash:** Requests are routed to a specific server based on the client's IP address, ensuring that the same client always connects to the same server.

In the context of real-time applications like chat apps, a key challenge is ensuring that users who are connected to different servers can still communicate seamlessly. This is often addressed by integrating a **shared state** (e.g., using Redis or a database) for communication between the servers.

Tools for Load Balancing in Node.js:

- **PM2 (Process Manager 2):** A popular process manager for Node.js that helps in clustering multiple instances of the Node.js app across multiple CPU cores. PM2 also supports load balancing in a simple manner.
- **Nginx:** A widely used web server that can act as a reverse proxy and load balancer for Node.js applications.
- **HAProxy:** Another powerful tool for load balancing, often used in enterprise environments.

Real-World Example: Scaling a Real-Time Chat Application

Let's walk through how you can scale a real-time chat application built with Node.js. This example will demonstrate the use of horizontal scaling, load balancing, and state management to handle a large number of users.

Scenario: You have a real-time chat application that allows users to send and receive messages in different chat rooms. As the user base grows, you need to ensure that the app can handle thousands of concurrent users without performance degradation.

1. **Setting Up Multiple Node.js Instances:** To scale the app horizontally, you'll run multiple instances of the Node.js server. This can be done using **PM2** to take advantage of multiple CPU cores and distribute the traffic between instances.

   Step 1: Install PM2:

   bash

   ```
   npm install pm2 -g
   ```

   Step 2: Start multiple instances:

   bash

   ```
   pm2 start app.js -i max   # Start as many
   instances as there are CPU cores
   ```

2. **Load Balancing with Nginx:** Nginx can be used as a reverse proxy to distribute incoming traffic to different Node.js instances.

   Step 1: Install Nginx: Follow your system's instructions to install Nginx (e.g., using `apt` on Ubuntu).

Step 2: Configure Nginx for load balancing: In the Nginx configuration file (`/etc/nginx/nginx.conf`), you can set up a basic round-robin load balancing configuration.

```nginx
nginx

http {
    upstream nodejs {
        server 127.0.0.1:3000;   # Node.js
instance 1
        server 127.0.0.1:3001;   # Node.js
instance 2
        server 127.0.0.1:3002;   # Node.js
instance 3
    }

    server {
        listen 80;

        location / {
            proxy_pass http://nodejs;
            proxy_http_version 1.1;
            proxy_set_header        Upgrade
$http_upgrade;
            proxy_set_header     Connection
'upgrade';
            proxy_set_header Host $host;
```

```
        proxy_cache_bypass
$http_upgrade;
        }
    }
}
```

Step 3: Restart Nginx:

```bash
bash
```

```bash
sudo service nginx restart
```

Now, Nginx will distribute requests to the available Node.js instances.

3. **Using Redis for Shared State (Pub/Sub for Chat Rooms):** Since we are scaling horizontally, we need a way for different Node.js instances to communicate with each other. Redis Pub/Sub can help us broadcast messages between different servers to ensure that all connected users in a chat room receive messages in real-time.

Step 1: Install Redis and Redis client for Node.js:

```bash
bash
```

```bash
npm install redis
```

Step 2: Set Up Redis Pub/Sub in Node.js: On each Node.js instance, you'll subscribe to Redis channels representing chat rooms.

javascript

```javascript
const redis = require('redis');
const subscriber = redis.createClient();
const publisher = redis.createClient();

// Subscribe to chat room channels
subscriber.subscribe('general');          // General chat room
subscriber.subscribe('sports');           // Sports chat room

// Handle incoming messages from Redis
subscriber.on('message',        (channel, message) => {
  console.log(`Received        message: ${message} in channel: ${channel}`);
  // Broadcast message to connected clients in the same chat room
});

// Example of publishing a message to a channel
publisher.publish('general',        'Hello, world!');
```

4. **Handling User Authentication and Sessions:** Since the app is now distributed across multiple servers, managing user sessions becomes crucial. A common approach is to use **JWT (JSON Web Tokens)**, as discussed in Chapter 7. Each user receives a JWT upon logging in, which is stored on the client side (usually in localStorage). This token is sent with each request to authenticate the user.

   Using JWT ensures that the server does not need to store session data, which makes scaling easier.

Conclusion

In this chapter, we learned how to scale real-time applications using Node.js, focusing on horizontal scaling, load balancing, and state management. By deploying multiple Node.js instances, using load balancers like Nginx, and leveraging Redis for shared state and pub/sub messaging, we can ensure that our real-time apps remain responsive and scalable as the user base grows.

Scaling real-time applications is an ongoing challenge, but with the right tools and techniques, you can ensure that your app can handle a large number of users without sacrificing performance or user experience. In the next chapters, we will continue to explore how to optimize and fine-tune these strategies for even larger applications.

CHAPTER 9

USING SOCKET.IO FOR REAL-TIME COMMUNICATION

Overview of Socket.IO in Node.js

Socket.IO is a powerful library for building real-time web applications in Node.js. It enables bi-directional communication between web clients and servers. Socket.IO is built on top of WebSockets and provides additional features like automatic reconnection, broadcasting, and multiplexing, making it ideal for real-time apps such as chat systems, live notifications, and collaborative tools.

Socket.IO consists of two main components:

1. **Server-side (Node.js):** The server-side component is used to handle connections from clients and emit events.
2. **Client-side (JavaScript):** The client-side component is used to connect to the Socket.IO server and handle incoming events.

Socket.IO operates over WebSockets but also falls back to other protocols (such as HTTP long-polling) when WebSockets are not supported. This makes it more robust, as it ensures real-time communication even in environments where WebSockets might be blocked or unavailable.

Key Features of Socket.IO:

- **Real-time Communication:** Facilitates instant message delivery between clients and the server.
- **Event-based Messaging:** Allows the server and clients to communicate via custom events, enabling easy handling of various types of messages.
- **Automatic Reconnection:** Socket.IO can automatically reconnect the client if the connection is lost, ensuring continuous communication.
- **Namespaces and Rooms:** Socket.IO allows grouping clients into "rooms," making it easy to send messages to specific sets of clients.

Real-Time Messaging with Socket.IO

Real-time messaging with Socket.IO is straightforward to implement. It allows the server to push messages to clients instantly, and clients can send messages back to the server in response. This makes it perfect for real-time applications like chat rooms, online gaming, and collaborative tools.

Setting Up a Basic Real-Time Chat with Socket.IO:

1. **Install Socket.IO:** To use Socket.IO in a Node.js application, you need to install both the server-side and client-side packages.

On the server-side (Node.js):

```bash
npm install socket.io
```

On the client-side (web page): Include the Socket.IO client-side library in your HTML:

```html
<script src="/socket.io/socket.io.js"></script>
```

2. **Creating a Socket.IO Server:** In your Node.js app, you can set up Socket.IO to listen for incoming connections and handle events.

Example of a basic Socket.IO server:

```javascript
const express = require('express');
const http = require('http');
const socketIo = require('socket.io');
```

```javascript
const app = express();
const server = http.createServer(app);
const io = socketIo(server);

// Serve the HTML page for the client
app.get('/', (req, res) => {
  res.sendFile(__dirname + '/index.html');
});

// Handle a connection event (when a client
connects)
io.on('connection', (socket) => {
  console.log('a user connected');

  // Listen for chat messages
  socket.on('chat message', (msg) => {
    console.log('Message received:', msg);
    io.emit('chat   message',   msg);   //
Broadcast the message to all clients
  });

  // Handle disconnection event
  socket.on('disconnect', () => {
    console.log('user disconnected');
  });
});

// Start the server on port 3000
server.listen(3000, () => {
```

```
console.log('Server       running      on
http://localhost:3000');
});
```

3. **Client-Side:** The client can connect to the server using Socket.IO and emit events to send messages or handle incoming events.

Example of a basic Socket.IO client (index.html):

html

```html
<!DOCTYPE html>
<html lang="en">
<head>
  <meta charset="UTF-8">
  <meta                    name="viewport"
content="width=device-width,        initial-
scale=1.0">
  <title>Real-Time Chat</title>
  <style>
    #messages { list-style-type: none; }
    input[type="text"] { width: 200px; }
  </style>
</head>
<body>
  <ul id="messages"></ul>
  <input id="m" autocomplete="off">
  <button
onclick="sendMessage()">Send</button>
```

```
<script
src="/socket.io/socket.io.js"></script>
  <script>
    var socket = io();

    // Listen for incoming messages from
the server
    socket.on('chat           message',
function(msg) {
      var            li            =
document.createElement('li');
      li.textContent = msg;

document.getElementById('messages').appen
dChild(li);
    });

    // Send a message to the server
    function sendMessage() {
      var         message            =
document.getElementById('m').value;
      socket.emit('chat          message',
message);
      document.getElementById('m').value =
'';
    }
  </script>
</body>
```

```
</html>
```

In this simple example:

- When a user types a message and clicks the "Send" button, it sends the message to the server via the `chat message` event.
- The server receives the message and broadcasts it to all connected clients.
- All connected clients receive the message and display it in real-time.

Broadcasting Events to Multiple Clients

One of the key features of Socket.IO is the ability to broadcast events to multiple clients at once. Broadcasting allows you to send a message to all connected clients or to a specific group of clients (e.g., users in the same chat room or a specific subset of users).

Broadcasting to All Clients: In the example above, the `io.emit()` function is used to broadcast a message to all connected clients. Every client connected to the server will receive the message and display it.

```
javascript
```

```
io.emit('chat message', msg); // Broadcasts to
all connected clients
```

Broadcasting to Specific Clients (Rooms): Socket.IO also supports "rooms," where clients can join specific channels or rooms and receive messages only for those rooms. This is useful for creating separate chat rooms or groups.

Example of Broadcasting to Specific Rooms:

```javascript
io.on('connection', (socket) => {
  // Client joins a specific room
  socket.on('join room', (room) => {
    socket.join(room);
    console.log(`User joined room: ${room}`);
  });

  // Send message to a specific room
  socket.on('chat message', (msg, room) => {
    io.to(room).emit('chat message', msg); // Broadcast to a specific room
  });
});
```

In this case:

- A client can join a room using `socket.join(room)`.

- When a message is sent, the server can use `io.to(room).emit('chat message', msg)` to broadcast the message only to clients in that room.

Real-World Example: Creating a Live Notification System with Socket.IO

Let's build a simple **live notification system** using Socket.IO. The goal is to notify all users in real-time when an event occurs (e.g., when a new user joins the platform or when a new update is available).

1. **Setting Up the Notification Server:** Here, we'll simulate sending a notification to all clients when a new user joins the platform.

javascript

```javascript
const express = require('express');
const http = require('http');
const socketIo = require('socket.io');

const app = express();
const server = http.createServer(app);
const io = socketIo(server);

// Serve the notification client
```

```
app.get('/', (req, res) => {
  res.sendFile(__dirname + '/index.html');
});

// Simulate sending notifications to all users
setInterval(() => {
  const notification = 'A new user has joined the
platform!';
  io.emit('notification', notification);
}, 5000); // Every 5 seconds

// Start the server
server.listen(3000, () => {
  console.log('Notification   server   running   on
http://localhost:3000');
});
```

2. **Client-Side:** On the client side, we will listen for the notification event and display the notifications in real-time.

html

```
<!DOCTYPE html>
<html lang="en">
<head>
  <meta charset="UTF-8">
  <meta   name="viewport"   content="width=device-
width, initial-scale=1.0">
```

```html
<title>Live Notifications</title>
<style>
  #notifications { list-style-type: none; }
  .notification { padding: 10px; border: 1px
solid #ddd; margin: 5px 0; }
</style>
</head>
<body>
  <h2>Live Notifications</h2>
  <ul id="notifications"></ul>

  <script
src="/socket.io/socket.io.js"></script>
  <script>
    var socket = io();

    // Listen for incoming notifications
    socket.on('notification', function(message)
{
      var li = document.createElement('li');
      li.classList.add('notification');
      li.textContent = message;

document.getElementById('notifications').append
Child(li);
    });
  </script>
</body>
</html>
```

3. **How It Works:**

   o The server sends a notification to all connected clients every 5 seconds (simulating the arrival of a new user).

   o The client listens for the `notification` event and adds the new notification to the list of displayed notifications.

Conclusion

In this chapter, we explored **Socket.IO**, a powerful tool for implementing real-time communication in Node.js applications. We learned how to set up a basic Socket.IO server and client, how to broadcast events to multiple clients, and how to create a real-time notification system. Socket.IO simplifies real-time communication, allowing developers to handle complex interactions like live messaging, notifications, and collaboration tools with ease.

Socket.IO provides an excellent solution for building responsive, low-latency applications that require real-time updates. In the next chapters, we will explore how to scale these systems and handle large numbers of simultaneous connections to ensure your real-time app can grow with your user base.

CHAPTER 10

UNDERSTANDING AND IMPLEMENTING REAL-TIME DATA STREAMS

What is a Data Stream in Real-Time Apps?

In the context of real-time applications, a **data stream** refers to a continuous flow of data that is delivered incrementally over time. Unlike traditional data retrieval methods where the client requests the entire dataset at once, a data stream allows data to be processed and transmitted in real-time, as it becomes available. This makes it ideal for scenarios where the application needs to handle real-time updates, such as live sports scores, stock prices, chat messages, or news updates.

Data streams are particularly useful in real-time apps because they:

- **Provide Continuous Updates:** Data is delivered continuously rather than in discrete chunks, allowing real-time processing and consumption.

- **Reduce Latency:** Since the data is available as soon as it's produced, applications can react immediately to new information.

- **Efficient Resource Usage:** Streaming allows data to be processed and transferred in smaller, more manageable chunks rather than loading large datasets all at once, which is resource-efficient.

Real-time data streaming is used in applications like:

- **Live video and audio streaming:** Platforms like YouTube or Twitch that stream media to users continuously.

- **Financial services:** Real-time stock prices and market data feeds.

- **Social media feeds:** Displaying continuous updates from various social networks.

- **News apps:** Streaming the latest headlines or breaking news.

Data streams ensure that applications stay up-to-date with the latest data without forcing users to refresh or request updates manually.

Using Streams in Node.js

In Node.js, streams are a powerful abstraction used to handle large volumes of data that are processed incrementally. A stream allows you to read or write data in chunks rather than loading the entire dataset into memory, making them efficient for working with large files, network requests, or any real-time data flow.

There are four types of streams in Node.js:

1. **Readable Streams:** Used for reading data, such as from a file or network socket.
2. **Writable Streams:** Used for writing data, such as writing to a file or sending data over a network.
3. **Duplex Streams:** Can be used for both reading and writing, such as HTTP request/response streams.
4. **Transform Streams:** A type of duplex stream that can modify or transform the data as it is written and read, such as compression or encryption.

Key Concepts of Streams in Node.js:

- **Flowing Mode vs. Paused Mode:**
  - In **flowing mode**, data is automatically sent as soon as it is available.
  - In **paused mode**, you have more control over when the data is read, typically done by explicitly calling .read() on the stream.

110

- **Backpressure:** When a writable stream cannot handle incoming data as fast as it is being written, backpressure occurs. Node.js manages this automatically to ensure smooth data flow.

- **Pipes:** The `pipe()` method is used to send the output of one stream to the input of another stream. This is commonly used when reading from one source (e.g., a file) and writing to another destination (e.g., a response or another file).

Example of Using a Readable Stream:

```javascript
const fs = require('fs');

// Create a readable stream from a file
const                readStream               =
fs.createReadStream('largefile.txt', 'utf8');

// Read data in chunks and process it
readStream.on('data', (chunk) => {
  console.log('Received chunk:', chunk);
});

// Handle end of the stream
readStream.on('end', () => {
  console.log('Stream ended');
});
```

In this example:

- We create a readable stream from a file and listen for the `data` event to process chunks of data as they arrive.
- The `end` event signals when the entire file has been processed.

Real-Time Data Streaming with Node.js

Node.js is particularly well-suited for real-time data streaming because of its non-blocking, event-driven nature. With streams, Node.js can efficiently handle large volumes of data, such as real-time sensor data, stock ticker updates, or live video/audio feeds, without blocking the event loop.

Real-Time Data Streaming Concepts:

1. **Stream Processing:** As data arrives in chunks, it is processed immediately (e.g., by transforming, filtering, or aggregating data).
2. **Event Emitters:** Streams in Node.js are event-driven, and events such as `data`, `end`, `error`, and `finish` allow you to handle different stages of the data flow.
3. **WebSockets and Streams:** Streams can also be used in combination with WebSockets to send real-time data to clients, ensuring low-latency updates.

112

Using WebSockets with Streams for Real-Time Communication: For example, you can stream data from a WebSocket server to multiple clients. In a real-time chat app, each message sent can be treated as a stream of data.

Example of Real-Time Data Streaming with WebSockets:

```javascript
const WebSocket = require('ws');
const fs = require('fs');

const wss = new WebSocket.Server({ port: 8080 });

// Simulate a real-time news feed by reading data
from a file stream
wss.on('connection', (ws) => {
  const                    readStream              =
fs.createReadStream('newsfeed.txt', 'utf8');

  readStream.on('data', (chunk) => {
    // Send each chunk as a message to the
connected client
    ws.send(chunk);
  });

  readStream.on('end', () => {
    console.log('Finished streaming news feed to
client');
```

```
  });

  ws.on('message', (message) => {
    console.log(`Received     from      client:
${message}`);
  });
});

console.log('WebSocket    server    running    on
ws://localhost:8080');
```

In this example:

- A **WebSocket server** is set up, and each client that connects receives real-time news updates streamed from a file.
- The `fs.createReadStream()` method is used to stream the file content, and each chunk of data is sent to the connected WebSocket client as it arrives.

Real-time data streaming enables the server to handle incoming data from a file (or other sources) and push updates to connected clients, maintaining a seamless experience with minimal delay.

Real-World Example: Implementing a Live Data Feed for a News App

In this example, we will implement a **live data feed** for a news application using Node.js streams and WebSockets. The goal is to stream the latest news headlines to clients in real-time, as new stories are added to a file or database.

Step 1: Set Up a Basic WebSocket Server: We will use WebSockets to establish a persistent connection between the server and clients, ensuring that news updates are pushed to all connected users as soon as they are available.

javascript

```javascript
const express = require('express');
const http = require('http');
const WebSocket = require('ws');
const fs = require('fs');

const app = express();
const server = http.createServer(app);
const wss = new WebSocket.Server({ server });

app.get('/', (req, res) => {
  res.sendFile(__dirname + '/index.html');
});

wss.on('connection', (ws) => {
```

```
  console.log('Client connected');

  // Create a stream of news data from a file
  const              newsStream              =
fs.createReadStream('newsfeed.txt', 'utf8');

  // Stream the data to the client
  newsStream.on('data', (chunk) => {
    ws.send(chunk); // Send each chunk to the
client
  });

  newsStream.on('end', () => {
    console.log('Finished streaming news');
  });

  ws.on('message', (message) => {
    console.log(`Received       from       client:
${message}`);
  });

  ws.on('close', () => {
    console.log('Client disconnected');
  });
});

server.listen(3000, () => {
  console.log('Server          running          on
http://localhost:3000');
```

```
});
```

Step 2: Client-Side Setup: The client will connect to the WebSocket server and display the news data as it arrives.

```
html
```

```html
<!DOCTYPE html>
<html lang="en">
<head>
  <meta charset="UTF-8">
  <meta name="viewport" content="width=device-width, initial-scale=1.0">
  <title>Live News Feed</title>
  <style>
    #news { list-style-type: none; padding: 0; }
    .news-item { padding: 10px; border: 1px solid #ddd; margin-bottom: 5px; }
  </style>
</head>
<body>
  <h2>Live News Feed</h2>
  <ul id="news"></ul>

  <script>
    const socket = new WebSocket('ws://localhost:3000');

    socket.onmessage = function(event) {
```

117

```
    const              newsItem              =
document.createElement('li');
    newsItem.classList.add('news-item');
    newsItem.textContent = event.data;

document.getElementById('news').appendChild(new
sItem);        `
    };

    socket.onopen = function() {
        console.log('Connected     to     WebSocket
server');
    };

    socket.onclose = function() {
        console.log('Disconnected   from   WebSocket
server');
    };
  </script>
</body>
</html>
```

Step 3: Simulate News Feed: For simplicity, the news data can be simulated by writing new lines to the newsfeed.txt file.

- As new headlines are added to the file, the server streams those headlines to the client in real-time.

118

Conclusion

In this chapter, we explored the concept of **real-time data streams** and how to implement them in Node.js using streams and WebSockets. We learned that data streams allow for continuous, low-latency delivery of information, which is essential for real-time applications. By combining streams with WebSockets, we can push real-time updates to clients, ensuring they always receive the latest data.

We also built a **live news feed** example, where data was streamed to clients as soon as new information became available. This approach is highly effective for real-time apps such as live news updates, sports scores, and financial data feeds.

In the next chapters, we will continue to explore more advanced techniques for optimizing and scaling these real-time systems.

CHAPTER 11

INTEGRATING DATABASES WITH NODE.JS FOR REAL-TIME APPS

Choosing the Right Database for Real-Time Apps (SQL vs. NoSQL)

When building real-time applications, one of the most important considerations is how to store and manage data. Depending on your application's needs, you might choose between a **SQL** (Structured Query Language) database or a **NoSQL** (Not Only SQL) database. Each type has its own strengths and weaknesses, and choosing the right one depends on your specific use case.

SQL Databases (Relational Databases):

- **Examples:** MySQL, PostgreSQL, SQLite
- **Structure:** SQL databases use structured schemas with tables, rows, and columns. They are great for handling structured data with predefined relationships (e.g., one-to-many, many-to-many).
- **ACID Compliance:** SQL databases are ACID (Atomicity, Consistency, Isolation, Durability)

compliant, making them ideal for applications that require strict data consistency and integrity.

- **Use Cases:** Ideal for applications that need to manage complex transactions, enforce strict data integrity, and rely on relational data (e.g., financial systems, e-commerce platforms).

NoSQL Databases:

- **Examples:** MongoDB, Redis, Cassandra, CouchDB
- **Structure:** NoSQL databases are more flexible in terms of data storage. They support various types of data models, including document-based (e.g., MongoDB), key-value (e.g., Redis), graph-based, and column-family stores.
- **Scalability:** NoSQL databases are designed for horizontal scaling, making them better suited for handling large amounts of unstructured or semi-structured data and for applications that need to scale quickly.
- **Use Cases:** Ideal for real-time apps, content management systems, and applications that need high availability and scalability, where data can change frequently and doesn't necessarily fit into a rigid schema.

For real-time apps, NoSQL databases like **MongoDB** are particularly attractive due to their scalability, flexibility, and ability to handle large volumes of concurrent, often unstructured, data.

Integrating MongoDB with Node.js

MongoDB is a popular NoSQL database that stores data in JSON-like documents, which makes it a natural fit for applications that need to store complex data structures. It is particularly well-suited for real-time applications due to its ability to handle large volumes of data with flexible schemas.

To integrate MongoDB with Node.js, you typically use the **Mongoose** library, which provides an elegant solution for interacting with MongoDB by offering a higher-level abstraction over the native MongoDB driver.

Steps to Integrating MongoDB with Node.js:

1. **Install MongoDB and Mongoose:** First, make sure that you have MongoDB installed on your local machine or use a cloud-based service like MongoDB Atlas. Then, install the mongoose package in your Node.js project:

   bash

   ```
   npm install mongoose
   ```

2. **Set Up MongoDB Connection:** To connect your Node.js application to MongoDB, use the `mongoose.connect()` method. Here's how to establish the connection:

```javascript
const mongoose = require('mongoose');

mongoose.connect('mongodb://localhost:270
17/realTimeApp', {
  useNewUrlParser: true,
  useUnifiedTopology: true,
}).then(() => {
  console.log('Connected to MongoDB');
}).catch((err) => {
  console.error('Error    connecting    to
MongoDB:', err);
});
```

In this example:

- The `realTimeApp` database is used. If it doesn't exist, MongoDB will create it for you.
- The `useNewUrlParser` and `useUnifiedTopology` options are to avoid deprecation warnings in MongoDB.

3. **Define a Schema and Model:** Next, you define a schema to model the data. In real-time applications, schemas can represent entities like users, messages, or chat rooms.

Example Schema for User Data:

javascript

```
const userSchema = new mongoose.Schema({
    username: { type: String, required: true,
unique: true },
    password: { type: String, required: true
},
    lastLogin:    {    type:    Date,    default:
Date.now },
});


const    User    =    mongoose.model('User',
userSchema);
```

In this example:

- o A userSchema is created to store user details.
- o The User model is based on this schema and is used to interact with the MongoDB users collection.

4. **Performing CRUD Operations:** With the User model, you can now perform Create, Read, Update, and Delete (CRUD) operations.

Example of creating a new user:

javascript

```
const newUser = new User({
  username: 'john_doe',
  password: 'password123',
});


newUser.save().then(() => {
  console.log('New user created!');
}).catch((err) => {
  console.error('Error   creating   user:',
err);
});
```

Example of retrieving user data:

javascript

```
User.findOne({    username:    'john_doe'
}).then((user) => {
  console.log('User found:', user);
}).catch((err) => {
  console.error('Error   fetching   user:',
err);
});
```

Real-Time Data Synchronization with Databases

Real-time data synchronization ensures that all clients connected to your application receive the latest data as soon as it's updated. This is crucial for applications like chat apps, social media platforms, or real-time dashboards, where users need to be kept in sync with the latest data without constantly refreshing their browsers.

How to Synchronize Data in Real-Time with MongoDB:

1. **Change Streams:** MongoDB offers **change streams** that allow you to listen for changes to documents in a collection. This feature is built on top of MongoDB's replication capabilities and is useful for implementing real-time data synchronization.

   Example of Listening for Changes with MongoDB Change Streams:

   javascript

   ```javascript
   const changeStream = User.watch();

   changeStream.on('change', (change) => {
     console.log('Change detected:', change);
     // Broadcast changes to clients using
   WebSockets or Socket.IO
   });
   ```

126

In this example:

- The `watch()` method listens for changes on the `User` collection.
- Whenever a change occurs (e.g., a new user is created or updated), the `changeStream` emits a change event that you can handle and broadcast to clients.

You can use this approach to push updates to clients instantly when something changes in the database, keeping all users in sync in real-time.

2. **Socket.IO and MongoDB Integration:** In a real-time chat app, for example, new messages can be stored in MongoDB, and updates can be broadcast to all connected clients using Socket.IO or WebSockets. When a message is inserted into the database, you can use a change stream to push it to all connected users.

Real-World Example: Managing User Data in a Real-Time App Using MongoDB

Let's implement a simple **real-time user management system** that handles user registration and login in a Node.js app. Whenever a new user is registered, we will broadcast this event to all connected clients in real-time, keeping everyone updated with the latest user information.

1. **Set Up Express and MongoDB Connection:** First, set up an Express server and connect to MongoDB, as shown in the earlier steps.

2. **User Registration and Login Routes:** Define routes to handle user registration and login.

```javascript
const express = require('express');
const bcrypt = require('bcryptjs');
const mongoose = require('mongoose');
const User = require('./models/user');
const app = express();

app.use(express.json());  // For parsing
JSON bodies

// User registration route
app.post('/register', async (req, res) =>
{
  const { username, password } = req.body;

  // Check if user already exists
  const userExists = await User.findOne({
username });
```

```
  if          (userExists)          return
res.status(400).send('User         already
exists.');

  // Hash the password
  const      hashedPassword    =    await
bcrypt.hash(password, 10);

  // Create and save the new user
  const newUser = new User({
    username,
    password: hashedPassword,
  });

  await newUser.save();
  res.status(201).send('User    registered
successfully!');
});

// User login route
app.post('/login', async (req, res) => {
  const { username, password } = req.body;

  const   user   =   await   User.findOne({
username });
  if          (!user)          return
res.status(400).send('User not found.');
```

```
const      isMatch      =      await
bcrypt.compare(password, user.password);
   if          (!isMatch)          return
res.status(400).send('Invalid
credentials.');

   res.send('Login successful!');
});

app.listen(3000, () => {
   console.log('Server      running      on
http://localhost:3000');
});
```

3. **Broadcasting New User Registration in Real-Time:**
   Use MongoDB change streams to watch for new user
   registrations and broadcast the event to connected clients
   using Socket.IO.

   Integrating Socket.IO with MongoDB Change Streams:

```javascript
const http = require('http');
const socketIo = require('socket.io');
const app = express();
const server = http.createServer(app);
const io = socketIo(server);
```

```
// Listen for user registration changes
const changeStream = User.watch();

changeStream.on('change', (change) => {
  if (change.operationType === 'insert') {
    const newUser = change.fullDocument;
    io.emit('newUser',    newUser);    //
Broadcast the new user to all connected
clients
  }
});

io.on('connection', (socket) => {
  console.log('New client connected');
});

server.listen(3000, () => {
  console.log('Server    running    on
http://localhost:3000');
});
```

4. **Client-Side:** On the client side, use Socket.IO to listen for the newUser event and display the new user in the UI.

Example Client-Side Code:

```
html
```

```
<script
src="/socket.io/socket.io.js"></script>
<script>
  const socket = io();

  socket.on('newUser', (user) => {
    console.log('New   user   registered:',
user);
    // Display the new user in the UI
  });
</script>
```

Conclusion

In this chapter, we explored how to integrate **MongoDB** with Node.js for real-time applications. We learned how to manage user data with MongoDB, perform CRUD operations, and use **MongoDB change streams** to synchronize data in real-time. We also demonstrated how to implement a simple real-time user management system with user registration, login, and live updates using **Socket.IO**.

Real-time data synchronization with MongoDB allows your application to stay up-to-date, ensuring that all connected clients receive the latest data without having to refresh their browsers. In the next chapters, we will continue to explore how to scale and optimize real-time applications using advanced techniques.

CHAPTER 12

BUILDING REAL-TIME APIS
WITH GRAPHQL

Introduction to GraphQL for Real-Time Data Querying

GraphQL is a powerful query language for APIs and a runtime for executing those queries with your existing data. Unlike REST, which requires you to define multiple endpoints for different resources, GraphQL allows clients to request exactly the data they need through a single endpoint. This makes it more efficient and flexible, especially for real-time applications.

Key Benefits of GraphQL for Real-Time Applications:

1. **Flexible Queries:** Clients can specify the exact fields they need in a query, reducing over-fetching and under-fetching of data.

2. **Single Endpoint:** GraphQL allows multiple resources to be accessed through a single endpoint, simplifying API design and usage.

3. **Real-Time Data Updates:** With GraphQL Subscriptions, clients can receive real-time updates when data changes,

making it perfect for applications like live sports scores, chat apps, and social media feeds.

4. **Strong Typing:** GraphQL uses a strongly typed schema, which provides a clear contract between the client and server, ensuring data consistency and reducing errors.

In real-time applications, GraphQL subscriptions allow clients to listen for changes to specific data in real-time, making GraphQL a perfect tool for live data feeds, such as sports scores, stock prices, or chat messages.

Setting Up a GraphQL API with Node.js

To set up a GraphQL API with Node.js, we will use the **Apollo Server** library, which is a popular GraphQL server implementation. We will also use **Express.js** to handle the HTTP server.

1. **Install Required Packages:** First, install the necessary packages for GraphQL and Apollo Server in your Node.js project:

```bash
npm install express apollo-server-express
graphql
```

2. **Create the GraphQL Schema:** In GraphQL, you define a **schema** that describes the data types, queries, and mutations that clients can request.

```javascript
const { gql } = require('apollo-server-express');

// Define your GraphQL schema
const typeDefs = gql`
  type Query {
    hello: String
    getUser(id: ID!): User
  }

  type User {
    id: ID
    name: String
    email: String
  }
`;
```

In this example:

- o The `Query` type defines the available queries. Here, `hello` is a simple query that returns a string, and `getUser` returns a user object based on the `id`.

135

- o The User type defines the structure of a user, including the id, name, and email.

3. **Create Resolvers:** A resolver is a function that fetches the data for a specific field in the schema.

javascript

```
const resolvers = {
  Query: {
    hello: () => 'Hello, world!',
    getUser: (parent, args) => {
      // Simulate fetching user data (e.g.,
from a database)
      return { id: args.id, name: 'John
Doe', email: 'john.doe@example.com' };
    },
  },
};
```

4. **Set Up Apollo Server and Express:** Now, set up the Apollo Server and integrate it with the Express.js server.

javascript

```
const express = require('express');
const { ApolloServer } = require('apollo-
server-express');

const app = express();
```

```
const server = new ApolloServer({
  typeDefs,
  resolvers,
});

async function startServer() {
  await server.start();
  server.applyMiddleware({ app });
  app.listen(4000, () => {
    console.log('Server      running      on
http://localhost:4000/graphql');
  });
}

startServer();
```

In this setup:

- o We create an **ApolloServer** instance using the typeDefs (schema) and resolvers (data fetching functions).
- o The server is then applied to an Express app, and the server starts listening on port 4000.

5. **Test Your GraphQL API:** Once the server is running, you can test it by visiting http://localhost:4000/graphql in a browser. This will open the Apollo GraphQL Playground, where

137

you can interact with your API by running queries and mutations.

Real-Time Subscriptions with GraphQL

GraphQL Subscriptions are a way to allow clients to receive real-time updates from the server. Subscriptions are similar to queries, but they are long-lived connections that allow the server to push updates to the client when data changes.

In the context of real-time applications, subscriptions are perfect for use cases like live chat, notifications, and real-time data feeds, such as live sports scores or stock price updates.

1. **Set Up a Subscription:** To implement subscriptions, you'll need to extend your schema to include a `Subscription` type. For example, you can subscribe to updates about a sports game or a user's status.

```javascript
const { gql } = require('apollo-server-express');

const typeDefs = gql`
  type Query {
    hello: String
```

```
}

type Subscription {
  scoreUpdated: Score
}

type Score {
  team: String
  points: Int
}
`;
```

2. **Implement Subscription Resolvers:** Subscription resolvers are a bit different from regular query resolvers. They use **Pub/Sub** (publish/subscribe) mechanisms to push updates to clients. You can use Redis, in-memory Pub/Sub, or other message brokers for this.

```javascript
const { PubSub } = require('apollo-server-express');
const pubsub = new PubSub();

const resolvers = {
  Query: {
    hello: () => 'Hello, world!',
  },
  Subscription: {
```

```
scoreUpdated: {
  subscribe:           ()            =>
pubsub.asyncIterator(['SCORE_UPDATED']),
  },
 },
};
```

In this example:

- o The `scoreUpdated` subscription will be triggered whenever a `SCORE_UPDATED` event is published to the PubSub system.
- o The `subscribe` function listens for the `SCORE_UPDATED` event and sends updates to the clients.

3. **Publishing Events:** You can publish events when certain actions happen on the server. For example, when a sports score is updated, you can publish a `SCORE_UPDATED` event, which will trigger the subscription and send the updated score to all connected clients.

```javascript
setInterval(() => {
  const score = { team: 'Team A', points:
Math.floor(Math.random() * 10) };
  pubsub.publish('SCORE_UPDATED',           {
scoreUpdated: score });
```

```
}, 5000);
```

In this example:

- o Every 5 seconds, a new score is generated and published to all subscribers.

Real-World Example: Creating a Live Sports Score API with GraphQL and Node.js

Let's create a real-world live sports score API that broadcasts updates to all clients using GraphQL subscriptions.

Step 1: Set Up the GraphQL Server (Same as above)

We have already set up the basic GraphQL server with subscriptions, and we'll use the same structure.

Step 2: Set Up the Subscription and Publishing Logic:

Add the logic to simulate live sports score updates and broadcast them to all clients via subscriptions.

```javascript
const { PubSub } = require('apollo-server-express');
const pubsub = new PubSub();
```

```
const typeDefs = gql`
  type Query {
    hello: String
  }

  type Subscription {
    scoreUpdated: Score
  }

  type Score {
    team: String
    points: Int
  }
`;

const resolvers = {
  Query: {
    hello: () => 'Hello, world!',
  },
  Subscription: {
    scoreUpdated: {
      subscribe:              ()                     =>
pubsub.asyncIterator(['SCORE_UPDATED']),
    },
  },
};

setInterval(() => {
```

```
  const score = { team: 'Team A', points:
Math.floor(Math.random() * 100) };
  pubsub.publish('SCORE_UPDATED',               {
scoreUpdated: score });
}, 5000);

const { ApolloServer } = require('apollo-server-
express');
const express = require('express');
const app = express();

const server = new ApolloServer({
  typeDefs,
  resolvers,
});

async function startServer() {
  await server.start();
  server.applyMiddleware({ app });
  app.listen(4000, () => {
    console.log('Server          running          on
http://localhost:4000/graphql');
  });
}

startServer();
```

Step 3: Client-Side Subscription:

On the client side, use Apollo Client or any GraphQL client that supports subscriptions to listen for real-time updates.

```javascript
import { ApolloClient, InMemoryCache,
ApolloProvider, gql } from '@apollo/client';
import { WebSocketLink } from
'@apollo/client/link/ws';

// WebSocketLink for subscriptions
const link = new WebSocketLink({
  uri: `ws://localhost:4000/graphql`,
  options: {
    reconnect: true,
  },
});

const client = new ApolloClient({
  link,
  cache: new InMemoryCache(),
});

const SCORE_UPDATED = gql`
  subscription {
    scoreUpdated {
      team
      points
    }
```

```
  }
`;

function App() {
  const    {    data,    loading    }    =
useSubscription(SCORE_UPDATED);

  if (loading) return <div>Loading...</div>;

  return (
    <div>
      <h2>Live Sports Score</h2>
      <p>{data.scoreUpdated.team}        -
{data.scoreUpdated.points} points</p>
    </div>
  );
}

export default () => (
  <ApolloProvider client={client}>
    <App />
  </ApolloProvider>
);
```

In this example:

- The **server** periodically generates and publishes new scores every 5 seconds using GraphQL subscriptions.

145

- The **client** subscribes to the `scoreUpdated` subscription and automatically updates the UI whenever a new score is received.

Conclusion

In this chapter, we explored how to use **GraphQL** to build real-time APIs with subscriptions. We covered how to set up a basic GraphQL server, implement subscriptions for real-time data updates, and create a live sports score API. By leveraging GraphQL and its powerful subscription system, we can easily provide real-time data updates to clients in a flexible and efficient way.

In the next chapters, we will explore how to optimize and scale GraphQL APIs to handle more complex use cases and larger volumes of real-time data.

CHAPTER 13

MONITORING AND DEBUGGING REAL-TIME NODE.JS APPS

The Importance of Monitoring and Debugging Real-Time Apps

Real-time applications are complex systems that need to handle many concurrent users, events, and data streams simultaneously. As a result, monitoring and debugging real-time Node.js applications are essential to ensure they function optimally and remain responsive under load. Real-time apps, such as messaging platforms, live feeds, or gaming servers, are sensitive to performance issues and bugs, as even small issues can negatively impact the user experience.

Why Monitoring and Debugging Are Crucial:

1. **Performance Issues:** Real-time apps need to be highly responsive. Delays, slowdowns, or high latency can lead to poor user experiences and a loss of engagement.
2. **Concurrency Problems:** With many concurrent users, real-time apps face challenges like race conditions, deadlocks, and data consistency problems that need to be tracked and resolved.

147

3. **Error Handling:** Real-time apps often interact with multiple services (e.g., databases, external APIs, WebSocket servers), and failure in one service can cause the entire app to malfunction. Effective error handling and monitoring are essential for identifying and fixing issues before they affect users.

4. **Scaling Challenges:** As your app grows and you scale to handle more users and requests, the complexity increases. Continuous monitoring is required to track the app's health, detect bottlenecks, and optimize resource usage.

Monitoring and debugging real-time Node.js apps is essential for maintaining a smooth user experience and preventing downtime. By using proper tools and techniques, you can ensure that your application remains stable, performs well under load, and provides a seamless experience to users.

Tools and Techniques for Debugging Node.js Apps

Node.js provides several tools and techniques for debugging, logging, and monitoring real-time applications. These tools help you identify performance bottlenecks, memory leaks, and errors, allowing you to fix issues before they impact users.

1. **Built-in Debugging Tools:** Node.js comes with a built-in debugger that allows you to step through code, inspect variables, and diagnose issues.

   Using Node.js Debugger:

   - To start the debugger, use the `inspect` flag when running your application:

   ```bash
   node --inspect app.js
   ```

   - This will open a debugging session in Chrome DevTools (accessible at `chrome://inspect` in the browser).
   - You can set breakpoints, inspect variables, and step through the code in real-time.

2. **Logging:** Effective logging is crucial for debugging, as it provides a way to trace issues and understand how the application behaves in production.

   Popular Logging Libraries:

   - **Winston:** A versatile logging library for Node.js that supports multiple log levels (e.g., `info`, `warn`, `error`) and transports (e.g., console, file, HTTP).

o **Morgan:** An HTTP request logger middleware for Express, useful for logging HTTP requests to help monitor traffic and troubleshoot issues.

o **Bunyan:** A fast JSON-based logging library for Node.js, useful for structured logging in production environments.

Example of using Winston for logging:

```javascript
const winston = require('winston');

const logger = winston.createLogger({
  level: 'info',
  transports: [
    new winston.transports.Console(),
    new          winston.transports.File({
filename: 'combined.log' })
  ]
});

logger.info('Application started');
logger.error('Something went wrong!');
```

3. **Profiling and Performance Monitoring:** Real-time apps require continuous monitoring to ensure they can handle many concurrent connections efficiently. Tools like

Node.js profiler and third-party monitoring solutions can help track performance and identify bottlenecks.

o **Node.js Profiler:** You can use the `--inspect` flag to enable performance profiling in Node.js.

```bash
```

```
node --inspect app.js
```

This allows you to monitor CPU usage and identify performance issues in real-time.

o **PM2:** PM2 is a process manager for Node.js that also provides features for monitoring the health and performance of applications, including real-time CPU and memory usage, and log aggregation.

o **New Relic:** A cloud-based application performance monitoring (APM) tool that provides insights into your app's real-time performance, including response times, error rates, and throughput.

4. **Error Handling:** Real-time applications need to handle errors gracefully to avoid crashes and disruptions. Node.js provides a built-in mechanism for catching uncaught exceptions and unhandled promise rejections.

151

Handling Uncaught Exceptions and Unhandled Rejections:

```javascript
process.on('uncaughtException', (err, origin) => {
  console.error(`Uncaught Exception: ${err.message}`);
  process.exit(1); // Exit the process after logging the error
});

process.on('unhandledRejection', (reason, promise) => {
  console.error(`Unhandled Rejection: ${reason}`);
  process.exit(1); // Exit the process after logging the error
});
```

- o **Custom Error Handling:** For real-time apps, custom error handling logic should be implemented to gracefully handle errors in services, like databases or WebSockets, and ensure that users get a proper response.

Setting Up Logging and Error Handling

Setting up proper logging and error handling is essential for debugging and monitoring real-time apps. Below, we will walk through setting up logging and error handling for a Node.js real-time chat app.

1. Setting Up Winston for Logging:

```javascript
const winston = require('winston');

// Create a logger with different log levels
const logger = winston.createLogger({
  level: 'info',   // Log level (info, warn, error)
  transports: [
    new winston.transports.Console({ format: winston.format.simple() }),
    new winston.transports.File({ filename: 'app.log' })
  ]
});

// Example usage of the logger
logger.info('Real-time chat app started');
logger.warn('User disconnected unexpectedly');
```

```
logger.error('Failed    to    connect    to    the
database');
```

2. Setting Up Custom Error Handling: In a real-time application, errors can occur at various points, such as when reading from a database, when a WebSocket connection fails, or when an unhandled promise rejection occurs. Handling errors properly ensures that the application can recover gracefully.

javascript

```javascript
// Express middleware for handling errors
app.use((err, req, res, next) => {
  logger.error(`Error                  occurred:
${err.message}`);
  res.status(500).send('Something went wrong!');

  // Send error notification to the monitoring
system (e.g., New Relic, Sentry)
  sendErrorNotification(err);
});

// WebSocket error handling
io.on('connection', (socket) => {
  socket.on('error', (err) => {
    logger.error(`Socket                  error:
${err.message}`);
    socket.emit('error', 'An error occurred');
  });
```

```
});
```

3. Monitoring Real-Time Data Flow with PM2: PM2 can be used to monitor real-time metrics of your Node.js application, including memory usage, CPU load, and process uptime.

```bash
bash
```

```
pm2 start app.js   # Start the app with PM2
pm2 monit          # Monitor the app's performance
in real-time
```

PM2 provides detailed information on memory consumption and CPU usage, allowing you to identify any performance issues that might occur under load.

Real-World Example: Monitoring and Debugging a Real-Time Node.js Chat App

Let's apply these monitoring and debugging techniques to a real-time chat application. The chat app uses WebSocket to allow multiple users to send and receive messages in real-time.

1. Logging User Events: We'll use Winston to log user events, such as when a user connects, sends a message, or disconnects. This will help us track activity and debug issues.

```javascript
javascript
```

```javascript
const winston = require('winston');
const io = require('socket.io')(server);

// Set up logging
const logger = winston.createLogger({
  level: 'info',
  transports: [
    new winston.transports.Console(),
    new   winston.transports.File({    filename:
'chatapp.log' })
  ]
});

// WebSocket connection event
io.on('connection', (socket) => {
  logger.info(`User connected: ${socket.id}`);

  socket.on('disconnect', () => {
    logger.info(`User              disconnected:
${socket.id}`);
  });

  socket.on('message', (message) => {
    logger.info(`Message        received        from
${socket.id}: ${message}`);
  });
});
```

2. Real-Time Monitoring with PM2: We can use PM2 to monitor our chat application's resource usage in real-time. If the app's CPU or memory usage spikes, we can track these issues and optimize performance.

bash

```
pm2 start chatapp.js  # Start the app with PM2
pm2 monit             # Monitor real-time
performance metrics
```

3. Error Handling: For real-time applications, we need robust error handling to catch any issues related to WebSocket connections, message sending, or database access. Here's how we can set up error handling in the chat app:

javascript

```
// WebSocket error handling
io.on('connection', (socket) => {
  socket.on('error', (err) => {
    logger.error(`WebSocket error on socket
${socket.id}: ${err.message}`);
    socket.emit('error', 'An error occurred,
please try again later.');
  });
});

// Global error handling middleware
```

```
app.use((err, req, res, next) => {
  logger.error(`Global error: ${err.message}`);
  res.status(500).send('Something went wrong!');
});
```

Conclusion

In this chapter, we explored how to effectively **monitor and debug real-time Node.js applications** using various tools and techniques. We discussed the importance of logging and error handling in ensuring that your app performs optimally and remains stable under load. We also demonstrated how to use tools like **Winston** for logging, **PM2** for performance monitoring, and proper error-handling strategies to ensure that real-time applications can be easily debugged and monitored.

By implementing these techniques in your real-time applications, you can ensure better performance, identify issues early, and provide a seamless experience for users. In the next chapters, we will continue to explore more advanced techniques for scaling, optimizing, and securing real-time apps.

CHAPTER 14

PERFORMANCE OPTIMIZATION IN REAL-TIME NODE.JS APPS

Optimizing Node.js for Performance

Node.js is designed for building high-performance, real-time applications. However, just like any other technology, optimizing Node.js for performance is essential to ensure your app can scale and handle increasing traffic and concurrent requests effectively.

Key Techniques for Optimizing Node.js Performance:

1. **Non-Blocking I/O:** Node.js is built on an asynchronous, non-blocking I/O model, which allows it to handle a large number of concurrent requests without blocking the main thread. This is ideal for real-time applications where multiple users might be sending requests simultaneously. The non-blocking I/O model ensures that the application remains responsive even under heavy load.

2. **Use of Event Loop:** The Node.js event loop is designed to handle multiple tasks concurrently by offloading operations to the background. For optimal performance, avoid long-running synchronous operations inside the

159

event loop, as they can block other requests and degrade performance.

3. **Minimize Memory Consumption:** Node.js is efficient, but memory usage can increase when handling large-scale applications or large amounts of data. Profiling and optimizing memory usage is important to ensure that your app does not run out of memory under heavy loads.

4. **Use Efficient Data Structures:** Choose the most appropriate data structures based on the operations you need to perform. For instance, using a hash map (or an object in JavaScript) is efficient for looking up items by key, while arrays are better for ordered data.

5. **Leverage Asynchronous Libraries:** For I/O-bound operations, make use of asynchronous libraries to prevent blocking the event loop. For instance, prefer using `fs.promises` for asynchronous file I/O instead of synchronous `fs.readFile()` calls.

Performance Profiling:

- **Node.js Profiler:** Use the built-in Node.js profiler (`--inspect` flag) to monitor the performance of your application. You can analyze CPU usage, memory consumption, and identify performance bottlenecks.

- **Chrome DevTools:** You can debug and profile your Node.js app using Chrome's DevTools by connecting to it via the Node.js inspector.

160

- **Third-Party Tools:** Tools like **New Relic**, **AppDynamics**, and **Datadog** can help monitor the performance of Node.js applications in production.

Using the Cluster Module for Performance Improvement

The **Cluster module** in Node.js allows you to take advantage of multi-core systems by forking multiple worker processes (each running an instance of the Node.js application). This is crucial for improving performance, particularly for CPU-bound tasks, as it enables Node.js to handle multiple requests simultaneously across multiple processes.

How the Cluster Module Works:

- The **master process** is responsible for creating child processes (workers), each of which is an instance of your Node.js application.
- The master process distributes incoming requests to the worker processes using the operating system's built-in load balancing mechanism.

Key Benefits of Using Clustering:

- **Improved Concurrency:** By utilizing multiple CPU cores, clustering allows Node.js to handle more simultaneous connections, making it suitable for high-traffic applications.

- **Fault Tolerance:** If one worker process crashes, others can continue to run without affecting the entire application.
- **Better Resource Utilization:** Clustering helps to take full advantage of multi-core processors, improving the performance of your application.

Setting Up Clustering in Node.js:

1. **Cluster Example:**

javascript

```javascript
const cluster = require('cluster');
const http = require('http');
const os = require('os');

const numCPUs = os.cpus().length;

if (cluster.isMaster) {
  console.log(`Master process is running
on PID: ${process.pid}`);

  // Fork workers
  for (let i = 0; i < numCPUs; i++) {
    cluster.fork();
  }
```

```
  // Restart worker if it dies
  cluster.on('exit',       (worker,      code,
signal) => {
    console.log(`Worker
${worker.process.pid} died`);
    });
} else {
  // Worker processes have a HTTP server
  http.createServer((req, res) => {
    res.writeHead(200);
    res.end('Hello, world!');
  }).listen(8000);

  console.log(`Worker process started with
PID: ${process.pid}`);
}
```

In this example:

- The master process forks multiple worker processes based on the number of CPU cores.
- Each worker process runs its own instance of the server, improving the app's concurrency.

2. **Using Cluster with WebSocket:** When using WebSockets for real-time communication, the clustering approach ensures that WebSocket connections are load

balanced across multiple worker processes, improving the app's scalability.

```javascript
const cluster = require('cluster');
const WebSocket = require('ws');
const http = require('http');
const os = require('os');

const numCPUs = os.cpus().length;

if (cluster.isMaster) {
  // Fork worker processes
  for (let i = 0; i < numCPUs; i++) {
    cluster.fork();
  }

  cluster.on('exit', (worker, code, signal) => {
    console.log(`Worker ${worker.process.pid} died`);
  });
} else {
  const server = http.createServer();
  const wss = new WebSocket.Server({ server });

  wss.on('connection', (ws) => {
```

```
    ws.send('Welcome   to   the   WebSocket
 server!');
   });

   server.listen(8080, () => {
      console.log(`Server   running   on   port
 8080 - Worker ${process.pid}`);
   });
 }
```

In this example:

- WebSocket connections are handled by worker processes, which helps distribute the load of handling multiple simultaneous WebSocket connections.

Caching Strategies for Real-Time Apps

Caching is essential for improving performance and reducing latency in real-time applications. By caching frequently accessed data, you can reduce the load on your databases and speed up data retrieval. Caching is particularly important in real-time apps that serve high-traffic requests, such as chat apps, gaming platforms, and news services.

Types of Caching:

1. **In-Memory Caching:**

- o **Redis** is a popular in-memory data store used to cache frequently accessed data in real-time applications.
- o It can store data in memory and provide fast access to it without querying a database for each request.
- o Redis also supports **TTL (Time-to-Live)** for automatic cache expiration, making it an ideal solution for real-time data.

Example of Using Redis for Caching:

javascript

```
const redis = require('redis');
const client = redis.createClient();

// Store data in cache
client.setex('news_headline',        60,
'Breaking   News:   Real-Time   Apps   are
Awesome!');

// Retrieve data from cache
client.get('news_headline', (err, data) =>
{
  if (data) {
    console.log('Cache hit:', data);
  } else {
    console.log('Cache miss');
```

```
    }
  });
```

2. **Database Query Caching:**
   - Cache results from expensive database queries that don't change frequently. For instance, caching the results of a popular query, such as fetching the top 10 trending articles or sports scores, can reduce the load on your database and speed up the response time.

3. **Content Delivery Networks (CDNs):**
   - For applications that involve large media files (e.g., videos, images), using a CDN can offload static content delivery to edge servers closer to the user, reducing latency.

Real-World Example: Optimizing a Live Video Streaming App

Let's look at a **live video streaming app** as an example of how to optimize real-time applications. A live video streaming app needs to handle a high volume of concurrent users and deliver data with minimal latency.

1. Use Clustering for Load Balancing:

- Use the **Cluster module** to distribute incoming WebSocket connections and HTTP requests across multiple Node.js worker processes.
- This ensures that the app can handle a large number of simultaneous connections without overloading a single server.

2. Caching Video Metadata and Thumbnails:

- **Redis** can be used to cache video metadata (e.g., title, description, number of views) and video thumbnails. This will reduce the load on the database and speed up access to frequently requested information.

```javascript
const redis = require('redis');
const client = redis.createClient();

// Cache video metadata
client.setex('video_123_metadata',        3600,
JSON.stringify({
   title: 'How to Optimize Node.js Apps',
   views: 5000,
}));
```

3. Implementing Efficient Video Delivery:

- Use a CDN to deliver video content efficiently to users around the world.

- For real-time streaming, implement a protocol like **HLS (HTTP Live Streaming)** or **WebRTC** for low-latency video delivery.

4. Monitoring Performance with PM2:

- Use **PM2** to monitor the performance of the app, track memory usage, CPU load, and identify any performance bottlenecks.

bash

```
pm2 start app.js --watch    # Start the app and
monitor for changes
pm2 monit                   # View real-time
performance metrics
```

Conclusion

In this chapter, we explored how to optimize Node.js real-time applications for performance. We discussed the importance of using the **Cluster module** to leverage multi-core systems, caching strategies with **Redis** to speed up data retrieval, and optimizing video streaming apps for scalability and performance. By implementing these strategies, you can ensure that your real-time applications remain responsive and scalable, even as they grow to handle more users and data.

In the next chapters, we will continue to build on these optimization techniques and explore how to ensure the reliability, security, and scalability of your Node.js real-time applications.

CHAPTER 15

IMPLEMENTING REAL-TIME NOTIFICATIONS

Real-Time Notifications in Web Apps

Real-time notifications are an essential feature in modern web applications. They allow the server to send instant alerts or updates to users, keeping them engaged with the application. Real-time notifications are widely used in applications like messaging platforms, social media, email systems, and e-commerce sites, where users need to be alerted about important events without having to constantly check for updates.

Why Real-Time Notifications Matter:

1. **User Engagement:** Real-time notifications keep users engaged by providing timely updates about important events, such as new messages, friend requests, or order status updates.

2. **Improved User Experience:** Users don't have to refresh the page or manually check for updates; they are instantly notified about important events.

3. **Business Value:** For businesses, real-time notifications can help in driving user actions, such as making a purchase, responding to a message, or completing a transaction.

Real-time notifications improve the overall user experience by creating a dynamic environment where the application reacts to user actions and events in real time. This is particularly important for web apps that require instant updates or alerts, such as e-commerce sites, social networks, or news websites.

Using WebSockets and Other Protocols for Notifications

There are several ways to implement real-time notifications in a web application, with WebSockets being one of the most commonly used protocols for bidirectional communication. However, other methods such as **Server-Sent Events (SSE)** and **Push Notifications** can also be used depending on the specific use case.

1. **WebSockets for Real-Time Notifications:** WebSockets provide a persistent connection between the server and client, allowing for real-time, bidirectional communication. When a notification needs to be sent, the server can push the message directly to the client, making

172

it ideal for real-time chat applications, live score updates, or real-time notifications.

Key Features of WebSockets:

o Persistent connection: Once established, the connection stays open, making it easy to send messages as events occur.

o Low latency: WebSockets allow the server to push messages immediately to the client without waiting for the client to request them.

Setting up WebSockets for Notifications:

o On the server, you'll create a WebSocket server that listens for incoming connections from clients.

o When an event occurs (e.g., a new message or order update), the server pushes a notification to all connected clients or specific clients.

Example:

```javascript

const WebSocket = require('ws');
const wss = new WebSocket.Server({ port: 8080 });
```

```
wss.on('connection', (ws) => {
  ws.send('Welcome to the notification
service!');

  // Sending a notification to the client
  setInterval(() => {
    ws.send('You have a new
notification!');
  }, 5000); // Send every 5 seconds
});
```

2. **Server-Sent Events (SSE):** SSE is a simpler method for sending notifications from the server to the client. Unlike WebSockets, SSE only allows the server to send updates to the client, not the other way around. SSE is ideal for use cases where the client only needs to listen for updates from the server, such as news feeds or stock price updates.

Advantages of SSE:

- o It's built on top of HTTP, so it's easier to set up and use compared to WebSockets.
- o It works well for one-way communication from server to client (e.g., notifications).

Setting up SSE:

```javascript
javascript
```

```
const express = require('express');
const app = express();

app.get('/events', (req, res) => {
  res.setHeader('Content-Type',
'text/event-stream');
  res.setHeader('Cache-Control',        'no-
cache');
  res.setHeader('Connection',        'keep-
alive');

  // Send a notification every 5 seconds
  setInterval(() => {
    res.write('data:   You    have   a    new
notification!\n\n');
  }, 5000);
});

app.listen(3000, () => {
  console.log('Server        running       on
http://localhost:3000');
});
```

3. **Push Notifications:** Push notifications are a form of notification that is sent from the server to the client even if the client is not currently interacting with the application. Push notifications are usually used in mobile apps or progressive web apps (PWAs) to alert users of

important updates when they are not actively using the app.

Key Benefits of Push Notifications:

- o **Cross-platform support:** Push notifications can be sent to mobile devices (iOS/Android) and browsers (Chrome, Firefox, Safari).
- o **Engagement:** Push notifications can help increase user engagement by alerting them to important updates, new content, or reminders.

How Push Notifications Work:

- o **Service Worker:** For web applications, push notifications are delivered via service workers that run in the background, even when the user is not actively using the web app.
- o **Push Service:** The server sends push messages to a push notification service (e.g., Firebase Cloud Messaging, Apple Push Notification Service) that forwards them to the client.

Real-World Example: Building a Real-Time Alert System for an E-Commerce Site

Let's implement a **real-time alert system** for an e-commerce site. The goal is to notify users about important events, such as a new order, a price drop on an item in their wishlist, or promotional offers.

Step 1: Set up the Notification System (Using WebSockets)

1. **Create a WebSocket Server:** We'll use WebSockets to push notifications to users in real time. When an important event occurs (e.g., a new order is placed), the server will push a notification to the relevant users.

   javascript

```javascript
const WebSocket = require('ws');
const wss = new WebSocket.Server({ port: 8080 });

wss.on('connection', (ws) => {
  console.log('User connected');

  // Simulate sending real-time alerts
(e.g., new order placed)
  setInterval(() => {
    ws.send('New order received! Check
your dashboard for more details.');
```

```
}, 5000); // Send every 5 seconds
});
```

2. **Client-Side Setup:** The client-side will be responsible for receiving these notifications and displaying them to the user.

```
html
```

```html
<script>
  const socket = new
WebSocket('ws://localhost:8080');

  socket.onmessage = function(event) {
    const notificationElement =
document.createElement('div');
    notificationElement.textContent =
event.data;

document.body.appendChild(notificationEle
ment);
  };
</script>
```

Step 2: Integrating Push Notifications (Optional)

For this real-world scenario, we can integrate **Push Notifications** to alert users even when they are not actively browsing the site.

This is ideal for notifying users about time-sensitive events like promotions, new orders, or stock updates.

1. **Request Permission for Push Notifications:** The client needs to request permission to show notifications.

```javascript
if ('Notification' in window &&
navigator.serviceWorker) {

Notification.requestPermission().then(per
mission => {
    if (permission === 'granted') {
        console.log('Push notifications are
enabled');
    }
  });
}
```

2. **Set Up a Service Worker:** The service worker will handle the background push notifications for the web app.

```javascript
if ('serviceWorker' in navigator) {

navigator.serviceWorker.register('/servic
e-worker.js').then(registration => {
```

```
    console.log('Service Worker registered
with scope:', registration.scope);
  });
}
```

3. **Push Notification Handling:** Inside the service worker file (service-worker.js), you'll define how the push notification will be displayed when the user is not actively using the app.

javascript

```
self.addEventListener('push', event => {
  const options = {
    body: event.data.text(),
    icon: '/images/notification-icon.png',
    badge:            '/images/notification-
badge.png'
  };


  event.waitUntil(

self.registration.showNotification('New
Offer!', options)
  );
});
```

Conclusion

In this chapter, we explored different techniques for implementing real-time notifications in web applications. We covered:

- **WebSockets** for bidirectional communication between the server and the client, enabling instant notification delivery.
- **Server-Sent Events (SSE)** for one-way communication from the server to the client, ideal for simple notifications.
- **Push Notifications** for sending alerts even when the user is not actively engaged with the web app, improving user engagement.

We also walked through a real-world example of building a real-time alert system for an e-commerce site, demonstrating how WebSockets and Push Notifications can be used to keep users informed about important events in real time.

By implementing these real-time notification strategies, you can keep your users engaged and ensure they are always up-to-date with the latest updates in your application. In the next chapters, we will continue to explore other aspects of building scalable and interactive real-time applications.

CHAPTER 16

REAL-TIME COLLABORATION FEATURES

Implementing Collaborative Features like Document Sharing and Editing

Collaborative features allow multiple users to interact with the same document or resource in real-time, making it possible for teams to work together seamlessly, even if they are in different locations. Examples of collaborative features include:

- **Document Sharing:** Allows users to share documents, images, or other types of media with others in real time. Changes made by one user should be visible to others immediately.

- **Real-Time Editing:** Multiple users can make edits to a document simultaneously, and these changes are instantly reflected on every user's screen.

- **Commenting and Annotation:** Users can add comments or annotations to specific parts of a document, and other users can see and reply to them in real time.

Real-time collaboration is essential for modern productivity tools like Google Docs, Microsoft Office 365, and collaborative design tools like Figma. The goal is to ensure smooth, low-latency interactions between users, enabling a seamless collaborative experience.

Real-Time Collaboration with WebSockets

WebSockets are ideal for implementing real-time collaboration features. WebSockets provide a bi-directional, full-duplex communication channel that allows the server to push updates to clients as soon as data changes, making them perfect for collaborative environments.

How WebSockets Help in Real-Time Collaboration:

1. **Instant Data Syncing:** WebSockets enable instant synchronization between clients. When a user makes a change to a document, the server can immediately broadcast the change to all connected clients, ensuring that everyone is working with the latest version.

2. **Event-Based Communication:** WebSockets allow for real-time communication of specific events (e.g., text edits, cursor movements, etc.) as they happen, which is essential for providing an interactive experience for all users.

3. **Scalability:** WebSockets are efficient in handling multiple users connected simultaneously, which is key when scaling collaborative applications.

Example of WebSocket Use in Real-Time Collaboration: In a collaborative note-taking application, when one user types or makes an edit, the changes are instantly sent to the server, which then broadcasts these changes to all connected users in the session.

Managing Concurrent Users in Collaborative Apps

Handling concurrent users effectively is one of the key challenges in building real-time collaborative apps. In such apps, you need to manage multiple users who may be editing the same document or interacting with the same data at the same time.

Challenges to Manage with Concurrent Users:

- **Data Consistency:** Ensuring that all users see the same version of the document at the same time.
- **Conflict Resolution:** Handling cases where two or more users make conflicting changes simultaneously.
- **User Presence:** Displaying which users are currently online, typing, or editing the document.
- **Performance:** Ensuring the system can scale to accommodate thousands or even millions of concurrent users without performance degradation.

Techniques for Managing Concurrent Users:

1. **Operational Transformation (OT):**
   o OT is an algorithm used in collaborative editing tools to ensure that all users see the same version of the document, even when multiple users are editing simultaneously.
   o It works by transforming the operations (e.g., text insertions or deletions) so that they can be applied in a consistent order, regardless of the sequence in which they were sent to the server.

2. **Conflict-Free Replicated Data Types (CRDTs):**
   o CRDTs are data structures that allow multiple users to make changes to the same document simultaneously without conflict.
   o CRDTs automatically resolve conflicts by ensuring that updates can be applied in any order and still result in a consistent final state.

3. **Versioning and Snapshots:**
   o Each edit or action by a user can be tracked as a version. The system can maintain snapshots of the document at various stages, allowing for rollback and comparison of different versions.

4. **User Presence and Event Handling:**
   o Real-time collaboration apps often implement presence features to show which users are actively editing the document. WebSockets can

be used to broadcast user status changes (e.g., when a user joins, leaves, or starts editing).

o For example, using WebSockets, you can emit an event when a user starts typing or when a user disconnects, keeping all users informed about the current state.

Real-World Example: Building a Real-Time Collaborative Note-Taking App

Let's walk through a real-world example of building a **real-time collaborative note-taking app** using Node.js and WebSockets. The app will allow multiple users to edit a shared document simultaneously, and changes made by one user will be immediately visible to all others.

Step 1: Set Up the WebSocket Server

We will use **Socket.IO**, a library built on top of WebSockets, to implement real-time communication between the server and the clients. The server will handle broadcasting edits to all connected users.

1. **Install the Required Packages:**

   bash

```
npm install express socket.io
```

2. **Create the Server:** Create a server that uses Socket.IO to broadcast real-time changes to the document.

```javascript
const express = require('express');
const http = require('http');
const socketIo = require('socket.io');

const app = express();
const server = http.createServer(app);
const io = socketIo(server);

app.get('/', (req, res) => {
  res.sendFile(__dirname + '/index.html');
});

let documentContent = '';  // Stores the
content of the document

io.on('connection', (socket) => {
  console.log('A user connected');

  // Send the current document content to
the new user
  socket.emit('document',
documentContent);
```

187

```
// Listen for document updates and
broadcast to all users
  socket.on('edit', (newContent) => {
    documentContent = newContent;
    io.emit('document', documentContent);
// Broadcast the updated content
  });

  socket.on('disconnect', () => {
    console.log('A user disconnected');
  });
});

server.listen(3000, () => {
  console.log('Server is running on
http://localhost:3000');
});
```

Step 2: Set Up the Client-Side

1. **Create an HTML Page for the Client:** The HTML page
   will allow users to edit a shared document, and their
   changes will be transmitted to the server and broadcast to
   all connected users.

```html
html

<!DOCTYPE html>
<html lang="en">
```

```html
<head>
  <meta charset="UTF-8">
  <meta                      name="viewport"
content="width=device-width,          initial-
scale=1.0">
  <title>Real-Time             Collaborative
Notes</title>
</head>
<body>
  <h1>Collaborative Note-Taking App</h1>
  <textarea         id="note"         rows="10"
cols="50"></textarea>

  <script
src="/socket.io/socket.io.js"></script>
  <script>
    const socket = io();

    // Listen for the current document
content from the server
    socket.on('document', (content) => {

document.getElementById('note').value     =
content;
    });

    // Emit changes to the server as the
user types
```

```
document.getElementById('note').addEventL
istener('input', () => {
    const          newContent          =
document.getElementById('note').value;
    socket.emit('edit', newContent);   //
Send the edited content to the server
  });
</script>
</body>
</html>
```

Step 3: Test the Application

1. Start the server by running `node app.js`.
2. Open `http://localhost:3000` in multiple tabs or different browsers.
3. As one user types into the `textarea`, the changes will be immediately reflected in all other clients connected to the app.

Conclusion

In this chapter, we explored how to implement **real-time collaboration features** like document sharing and editing in a Node.js app using **WebSockets** (via Socket.IO). We learned how to handle concurrent users by broadcasting updates to all connected clients and how to manage real-time collaboration by sending live updates whenever a user edits the document.

We also discussed techniques for handling concurrency and ensuring that users can work on the same document without conflicts. This real-time collaboration example is just the beginning of building collaborative applications; you can extend these concepts to more complex scenarios like collaborative drawing, live code editing, or interactive whiteboards.

In the next chapters, we will dive deeper into optimizing collaborative features and discuss how to scale these systems to handle millions of concurrent users efficiently.

CHAPTER 17

USING MICROSERVICES ARCHITECTURE FOR REAL-TIME APPS

Introduction to Microservices Architecture

Microservices architecture is a modern approach to designing and building applications where the system is broken down into smaller, independent services. Each service is focused on a specific business functionality and communicates with other services through APIs (typically REST or messaging protocols). This contrasts with traditional monolithic architecture, where the entire application is built as a single, tightly coupled unit.

Key Characteristics of Microservices:

1. **Independent Services:** Each microservice is responsible for a specific feature or piece of functionality.
2. **Decentralized Data Management:** Each service manages its own database, ensuring loose coupling between services.

3. **Communication Through APIs:** Microservices interact with each other via lightweight communication protocols, such as HTTP, WebSockets, or message brokers.

4. **Autonomy and Scalability:** Each service can be developed, deployed, and scaled independently, making it easier to maintain and update the system.

Microservices are an excellent fit for **real-time applications** because they allow you to isolate different parts of your app (e.g., notifications, user management, messaging, etc.), making it easier to scale, manage, and update individual components without disrupting the entire system.

How to Structure Real-Time Apps with Microservices

In a **real-time application**, different services might be responsible for different tasks. For example, in a chat application, one service might handle user authentication, another service might manage messages, and another might deal with notifications. Using microservices architecture helps in structuring these real-time apps in a more modular and scalable way.

Here's how to structure real-time apps using microservices:

1. **Breaking Down the Application into Services:**

- o **User Service:** Responsible for user management (e.g., login, registration, user profile).

- o **Messaging Service:** Handles real-time messaging, such as sending and receiving messages.

- o **Notification Service:** Pushes notifications to users when new events happen (e.g., a new message, a friend request).

- o **Media Service:** Manages media uploads and streaming (e.g., images, videos).

- o **Search Service:** Provides real-time search for content or users.

2. **Choosing Communication Protocols:** Microservices need to communicate with each other. The most common communication methods include:

    - o **RESTful APIs:** For synchronous communication between services.

    - o **Message Brokers (e.g., Kafka, RabbitMQ):** For asynchronous communication, where one service publishes messages and others consume them. This is especially useful for real-time applications to decouple services and ensure high availability.

3. **Handling Real-Time Data:** Real-time applications require fast data transmission and processing. WebSockets or **Server-Sent Events (SSE)** are typically

used for communication between services and clients. For instance:

- o The **Messaging Service** might use WebSockets to broadcast messages to users in real time.
- o The **Notification Service** might use WebSockets or push notifications to alert users about new activities.

4. **Service Discovery and Load Balancing:** In a microservices-based real-time app, you might have multiple instances of the same service running in parallel to handle scalability. **Service discovery** and **load balancing** are critical to ensure that requests are routed to the appropriate instances. Tools like **Kubernetes** and **Docker Swarm** can help manage service scaling and load balancing.

5. **Database Management:** Each microservice manages its own database, which helps ensure loose coupling between services. For real-time applications, consider using:

- o **NoSQL Databases (e.g., MongoDB, Redis):** For storing unstructured or semi-structured data like chat messages or social media posts.
- o **SQL Databases (e.g., PostgreSQL, MySQL):** For structured data where relationships between entities are important.

Benefits and Challenges of Microservices in Real-Time Applications

Benefits of Microservices in Real-Time Apps:

1. **Scalability:** Each microservice can be scaled independently based on its load. For example, the messaging service can be scaled up during peak traffic, without needing to scale the entire application.

2. **Flexibility:** Microservices allow you to use the best technology for each service. For example, you might use WebSockets in the messaging service for real-time communication, while using a REST API for user authentication.

3. **Resilience and Fault Isolation:** Since microservices are independent, failures in one service do not necessarily affect others. This makes the system more resilient to outages.

4. **Faster Development and Deployment:** Teams can work on individual services independently, allowing for faster development cycles and easier deployment. You can release updates for one service without needing to redeploy the entire app.

Challenges of Microservices in Real-Time Apps:

1. **Complexity in Management:** Managing a microservices architecture can be complex, especially as the number of

services grows. You'll need tools for service discovery, API gateways, and centralized logging.

2. **Data Consistency:** Since each microservice has its own database, maintaining data consistency across services can be challenging, particularly in real-time applications that require up-to-date data.

3. **Latency:** Asynchronous communication between services, especially using message brokers, can introduce latency. In a real-time application, this could impact the user experience.

4. **Deployment Overhead:** Microservices require a well-structured deployment pipeline. Managing and deploying many services in a distributed environment requires tools like Kubernetes, Docker, or orchestration platforms to handle service management and scaling.

Real-World Example: Building a Real-Time Social Media Platform Using Microservices

Let's create a **real-time social media platform** with microservices architecture. The platform will allow users to post content, like and comment on posts, send messages to friends, and receive notifications in real-time.

Services Breakdown:

1. **User Service:** Handles user authentication, profiles, and friend requests.

2. **Post Service:** Manages user posts, likes, and comments.

3. **Messaging Service:** Allows users to send and receive direct messages.

4. **Notification Service:** Sends real-time notifications for new messages, likes, and comments.

5. **Feed Service:** Provides a real-time feed of posts for each user.

Step 1: Set Up the User Service

The User Service manages user registration and authentication, using JWT tokens to authenticate requests.

```javascript
// user-service.js
const express = require('express');
const jwt = require('jsonwebtoken');
const app = express();
const PORT = 5000;


app.use(express.json());

// User registration route
app.post('/register', (req, res) => {
  const { username, password } = req.body;
  // Simulate saving user to the database
```

```javascript
const user = { id: 1, username, password };

// Create JWT token
const token = jwt.sign(user, 'secret_key');
res.json({ token });
});


// Start the user service server
app.listen(PORT, () => {
  console.log(`User service running on
http://localhost:${PORT}`);
});
```

Step 2: Set Up the Post Service

The Post Service allows users to create posts, like posts, and comment on posts. It broadcasts new posts and interactions to the Notification Service in real time.

javascript

```javascript
// post-service.js
const express = require('express');
const app = express();
const PORT = 6000;


app.use(express.json());


// Simulate in-memory storage for posts
let posts = [];
```

```
// Create a new post
app.post('/post', (req, res) => {
  const { userId, content } = req.body;
  const newPost = { id: posts.length + 1, userId,
content };
  posts.push(newPost);
  res.json(newPost);
  // Notify the notification service about the
new post
  // In a real app, this would be done via a
messaging queue (e.g., RabbitMQ)
  notifyNewPost(newPost);
});

// Simulate notification of a new post
function notifyNewPost(post) {
  // Simulate broadcasting the post to a
notification service
  console.log('Broadcasting new post:', post);
}

app.listen(PORT, () => {
  console.log(`Post       service       running       on
http://localhost:${PORT}`);
});
```

Step 3: Set Up the Messaging Service

The Messaging Service handles real-time chat messages between users. We'll use **WebSockets** to allow real-time communication.

```
javascript
```

```javascript
// messaging-service.js
const WebSocket = require('ws');
const wss = new WebSocket.Server({ port: 7000 });

wss.on('connection', (ws) => {
  console.log('User connected');
  ws.on('message', (message) => {
    console.log(`Received message: ${message}`);
    ws.send(`Message received: ${message}`);
  });
});

console.log('Messaging    service    running    on
ws://localhost:7000');
```

Step 4: Set Up the Notification Service

The Notification Service is responsible for notifying users about new posts, comments, likes, or messages. We'll use WebSockets to push these notifications to connected users in real time.

```
javascript
```

```javascript
// notification-service.js
```

201

```
const WebSocket = require('ws');
const wss = new WebSocket.Server({ port: 8000 });

wss.on('connection', (ws) => {
  console.log('Notification    service:    User
connected');
  ws.on('message', (message) => {
    console.log(`Received         notification:
${message}`);
  });
});

console.log('Notification   service   running   on
ws://localhost:8000');
```

Step 5: Connect the Microservices

Each service communicates using HTTP, WebSockets, or a message broker (e.g., **RabbitMQ** or **Kafka**) to send messages and updates between services. For example, when a new post is created in the Post Service, it sends a notification to the Notification Service, which then pushes updates to the clients.

Conclusion

In this chapter, we explored how to build real-time applications using **microservices architecture**. We covered:

- Breaking down a real-time app into independent services, such as user management, post handling, messaging, and notifications.
- How each microservice can operate independently and communicate with others via APIs or message brokers.
- The challenges and benefits of using microservices in real-time applications, including scalability, fault tolerance, and flexibility.
- A **real-world example** of building a **real-time social media platform**, which uses microservices to handle user interactions, posts, messaging, and notifications.

Microservices architecture provides a powerful way to build scalable, flexible, and resilient real-time applications. In the next chapters, we will continue to explore more advanced techniques for optimizing and scaling these real-time systems.

CHAPTER 18

HANDLING REAL-TIME AUDIO AND VIDEO STREAMING

Introduction to Real-Time Media Streaming

Real-time media streaming refers to the process of transmitting audio, video, or other multimedia content from one device to another in real-time. Unlike traditional streaming services where content is pre-recorded and played back to the user, real-time media streaming involves continuous transmission of data as it is captured or generated.

Real-time media streaming is widely used in applications like video calls, online meetings, live broadcasting, and gaming. Some common use cases include:

- **Video Conferencing:** Platforms like Zoom or Google Meet that allow multiple users to engage in live video chats.
- **Online Gaming:** Games that require real-time video or audio communication between players.

- **Live Streaming:** Broadcasts where viewers can interact in real-time with the stream, such as live events or social media streaming.

Building real-time audio and video streaming applications presents several challenges, including managing network bandwidth, ensuring synchronization of audio and video streams, and maintaining high-quality media transmission with low latency.

Setting up WebRTC with Node.js for Video Chat

WebRTC (Web Real-Time Communication) is an open-source project that enables real-time communication (audio, video, and data) directly between browsers without the need for plugins. It allows applications to establish peer-to-peer connections, making it perfect for building real-time video and audio chat applications.

Key WebRTC Features:

1. **Peer-to-Peer Communication:** WebRTC allows direct communication between clients, reducing the need for a central server for media transmission (though signaling and connection establishment may still require a server).
2. **Real-Time Audio and Video:** WebRTC handles real-time transmission of audio and video streams between peers.

3. **Data Channels:** WebRTC supports data channels, allowing peers to exchange arbitrary data (e.g., files, text chat) in addition to audio and video.

Components of WebRTC:

1. **MediaStream:** Represents the media (audio or video) being transmitted.
2. **RTCPeerConnection:** Manages the communication session between peers, establishing the connection and handling the transmission of audio, video, and data.
3. **RTCDataChannel:** Allows peers to exchange data (e.g., files, messages) in real-time.

Steps to Set Up WebRTC with Node.js:

1. **Install WebRTC Dependencies:** To get started, you'll need to set up a signaling server. We will use **Socket.IO** to handle the signaling process (i.e., the process of establishing and maintaining the connection between peers).

   Install the necessary packages:

   ```bash
   npm install express socket.io
   ```

2. **Create the Signaling Server with Socket.IO:** The signaling server handles the exchange of messages (such as `offer`, `answer`, and `ICE candidates`) between peers to establish the WebRTC connection.

```javascript
const express = require('express');
const http = require('http');
const socketIo = require('socket.io');

const app = express
```

A network error occurred. Please check your connection and try again. If this issue persists please contact us through our help center at help.openai.com.

CHAPTER 1

HANDLING REAL-TIME WEBSOCKETS WITH SECURITY IN MIND

Securing WebSocket Connections

WebSocket connections are inherently different from traditional HTTP connections, as they maintain an open and persistent connection between the client and the server. While this persistence is crucial for real-time communication, it also poses security risks. WebSocket connections can be vulnerable to threats like man-in-the-middle (MITM) attacks, unauthorized access, and data breaches if not properly secured.

Here are some key strategies for securing WebSocket connections:

1. **Use Secure WebSocket Protocol (WSS):** The first step in securing WebSocket connections is to use the secure WebSocket protocol (`wss://`) instead of the unencrypted version (`ws://`). This ensures that all data transmitted

between the client and the server is encrypted, protecting it from eavesdropping and tampering.

Example:

```javascript
```

```javascript
const WebSocket = require('ws');
const server = new WebSocket.Server({
  port: 8080,
  secure: true    // Enforces secure
WebSocket (WSS) connections
});
```

2. **Enforce Secure Origin:** To mitigate cross-origin attacks, you should ensure that your WebSocket server only accepts connections from trusted origins. This is particularly important when dealing with cross-origin WebSocket connections.

Example (Enforcing Origin):

```javascript
```

```javascript
const wss = new WebSocket.Server({
  port: 8080,
  handleProtocols: (protocols, request) =>
{
```

```
if      (request.headers.origin    ===
'https://trusted-domain.com') {
    return true; // Allow the connection
    }
    return false; // Reject the connection
  }
});
```

3. **Use WebSocket Subprotocols:** WebSocket subprotocols can be used to ensure that the client and server agree on the communication format and behavior. This helps in preventing unauthorized or malicious clients from establishing connections.

   Example (Subprotocols):

   javascript

```
const wss = new WebSocket.Server({
  port: 8080,
  perMessageDeflate: true,
  handleProtocols: (protocols) => {
    return      protocols.includes('chat-
protocol'); // Accept only the desired
protocol
  }
});
```

Implementing SSL/TLS for Encrypted Connections

To ensure that data transmitted over WebSockets is secure, you need to implement SSL/TLS encryption. This can be done by using **WSS** (WebSocket Secure), which runs on top of SSL/TLS, just like HTTPS does for regular HTTP.

Steps to Implement SSL/TLS for WSS:

1. **Obtain an SSL/TLS Certificate:** You can obtain a certificate from a trusted Certificate Authority (CA) or create a self-signed certificate (for development purposes).

   Example of a self-signed certificate (for testing purposes):

   ```bash
   openssl req -new -newkey rsa:2048 -days 365
   -nodes -x509 -keyout server-key.pem -out
   server-cert.pem
   ```

2. **Set Up SSL/TLS in Node.js WebSocket Server:** To enable SSL/TLS, you need to use the `https` module in Node.js along with WebSocket. This will allow the server to handle encrypted WebSocket connections (`wss://`).

   Example of Setting Up WSS:

211

```javascript
const https = require('https');
const fs = require('fs');
const WebSocket = require('ws');

const server = https.createServer({
  key: fs.readFileSync('server-key.pem'),
  cert: fs.readFileSync('server-cert.pem')
});

const wss = new WebSocket.Server({ server
});

wss.on('connection', (ws) => {
  console.log('Secure WebSocket connection
established');
  ws.on('message', (message) => {
    console.log('Received:', message);
  });
});

server.listen(8080, () => {
  console.log('Server        running        at
https://localhost:8080');
});
```

3. **Force HTTPS:** Ensure that your WebSocket server can only be accessed over HTTPS by redirecting HTTP traffic

to HTTPS. This prevents connections to your WebSocket server over insecure channels.

```javascript
const http = require('http');

const httpServer = http.createServer((req, res) => {
  res.writeHead(301, { 'Location': 'https://' + req.headers.host + req.url });
  res.end();
});

httpServer.listen(80); // Redirect all HTTP requests to HTTPS
```

Authenticating WebSocket Connections with JWT

WebSocket connections are persistent, and by default, they don't have a built-in authentication mechanism. This makes it essential to secure the WebSocket connection by ensuring that only authenticated users can establish a connection.

One effective way to authenticate WebSocket connections is by using **JSON Web Tokens (JWT)**. JWT allows you to authenticate users on initial connection and verify their identity before permitting data exchange.

Steps to Implement JWT Authentication for WebSockets:

1. **Authenticate User and Issue JWT:** When a user logs in, issue a JWT that includes the user's information and any relevant permissions or roles. The client stores this token and sends it to the server when attempting to establish a WebSocket connection.

   Example of JWT Authentication in Node.js:

   ```javascript
   const jwt = require('jsonwebtoken');

   // Issue JWT after successful login
   app.post('/login', (req, res) => {
     const username = req.body.username;
     const user = { id: 1, username }; // Simulated user data
     const token = jwt.sign(user, 'secret-key', { expiresIn: '1h' });
     res.json({ token });
   });
   ```

2. **Verify JWT on WebSocket Connection:** When a client attempts to connect via WebSocket, send the JWT token along with the connection request. On the server, intercept the WebSocket connection and verify the token before allowing the client to join.

Example of JWT Authentication for WebSocket:

javascript

```javascript
const WebSocket = require('ws');
const jwt = require('jsonwebtoken');

const wss = new WebSocket.Server({ port: 8080 });

wss.on('connection', (ws, req) => {
  const token = req.headers['authorization']?.split(' ')[1]; // Get JWT from Authorization header

  if (!token) {
    ws.close(); // Close connection if no token is provided
    return;
  }

  jwt.verify(token, 'secret-key', (err, decoded) => {
    if (err) {
      ws.close(); // Close connection if token is invalid
      return;
    }
```

```
    // Authentication successful, user can
now send/receive messages
    console.log('User    authenticated:',
decoded.username);
    ws.on('message', (message) => {
      console.log('Received:', message);
    });
  });
});
```

3. **Client-Side WebSocket Connection:** The client sends the JWT in the `Authorization` header when initiating the WebSocket connection.

Example of Sending JWT with WebSocket:

javascript

```
const token = localStorage.getItem('jwt');
// Assume JWT is stored in localStorage

const         ws         =         new
WebSocket('wss://localhost:8080', {
  headers: {
    'Authorization': `Bearer ${token}`
  }
});

ws.onopen = () => {
```

```
    console.log('WebSocket          connection
    established');
    };

    ws.onmessage = (event) => {
      console.log('Received:', event.data);
    };
```

Real-World Example: Secure Real-Time Chat with End-to-End Encryption

Let's walk through an example of building a **secure real-time chat app** using **WebSockets, SSL/TLS encryption**, and **JWT authentication**. This chat app will use WebSocket connections for real-time messaging and implement **end-to-end encryption** (E2EE) to ensure that messages are only readable by the sender and receiver.

Step 1: Set Up Secure WebSocket Server We will use **SSL/TLS** to secure the WebSocket connections and **JWT** for authenticating users before they can send or receive messages.

javascript

```javascript
const https = require('https');
const fs = require('fs');
const WebSocket = require('ws');
const jwt = require('jsonwebtoken');
```

```
const server = https.createServer({
  key: fs.readFileSync('server-key.pem'),
  cert: fs.readFileSync('server-cert.pem')
});

const wss = new WebSocket.Server({ server });

wss.on('connection', (ws, req) => {
  const                    token                    =
req.headers['authorization']?.split(' ')[1];

  if (!token) {
    ws.close(); // Close connection if no token
    return;
  }

  jwt.verify(token, 'secret-key', (err, decoded)
=> {
    if (err) {
      ws.close(); // Close connection if token is
invalid
      return;
    }

    console.log('Authenticated          user:',
decoded.username);
```

```javascript
    // Real-time chat functionality with end-to-
end encryption (E2EE)
    ws.on('message', (encryptedMessage) => {
        const           decryptedMessage        =
decryptMessage(encryptedMessage);     //     Decrypt
message
        console.log('Received              message:',
decryptedMessage);

        // Broadcast encrypted message to all other
connected users
        wss.clients.forEach(client => {
            if (client !== ws && client.readyState
=== WebSocket.OPEN) {
                const      encryptedResponse       =
encryptMessage('Hello, ' + decoded.username);
                client.send(encryptedResponse);    //
Send encrypted message to other clients
            }
        });
    });
  });
});


// Function to simulate encryption
function encryptMessage(message) {
  return
Buffer.from(message).toString('base64');     //
```

Simple base64 encryption (for illustration purposes)
}

```
// Function to simulate decryption
function decryptMessage(encryptedMessage) {
  return          Buffer.from(encryptedMessage,
'base64').toString('utf-8');
}

server.listen(8080, () => {
  console.log('Secure  WebSocket  server  running
on wss://localhost:8080');
});
```

Step 2: Client-Side Setup for Secure Chat On the client-side, users will authenticate via JWT and use WebSocket for encrypted real-time communication.

html

```
<!DOCTYPE html>
<html lang="en">
<head>
  <meta charset="UTF-8">
  <meta  name="viewport"  content="width=device-
width, initial-scale=1.0">
  <title>Secure Real-Time Chat</title>
</head>
```

```html
<body>
  <h2>Secure Chat</h2>
  <input id="message" type="text"
placeholder="Type your message here" />
  <button onclick="sendMessage()">Send</button>

  <script>
    const token = 'your_jwt_token_here';    //
Example: Get JWT from local storage or login API
    const ws = new
WebSocket('wss://localhost:8080', {
      headers: { 'Authorization': `Bearer
${token}` }
    });

    ws.onopen = () => {
      console.log('WebSocket          connection
established');
    };

    ws.onmessage = (event) => {
      const decryptedMessage = atob(event.data);
// Decrypt the message
      console.log('Received:',
decryptedMessage);
    };

    function sendMessage() {
```

221

```
    const          message          =
document.getElementById('message').value;
    const encryptedMessage = btoa(message); //
Encrypt the message using base64 (for simplicity)
    ws.send(encryptedMessage);
  }
 </script>
</body>
</html>
```

Step 3: Testing the Secure Chat Application

1. Run the WebSocket server (node server.js).
2. Open the chat app in multiple browsers or tabs.
3. Send a message, and the encrypted content will be transmitted securely via WebSocket.
4. The message will be decrypted only by the recipient, ensuring **end-to-end encryption**.

Conclusion

In this chapter, we explored how to implement **secure WebSocket connections** using **SSL/TLS encryption** and **JWT authentication**. We also discussed how to manage real-time communication with **WebSockets**, ensuring the security of sensitive data through **end-to-end encryption**.

We walked through a **real-world example** of building a **secure real-time chat app** with WebSocket and JWT, demonstrating the importance of authentication and encryption in real-time applications. By securing WebSocket connections and encrypting messages, you can build secure, privacy-conscious real-time apps.

In the next chapters, we will explore additional techniques for securing real-time applications, such as rate limiting, API security, and further strategies for scaling and optimizing WebSocket-based systems.

CHAPTER 20

REAL-TIME APP DEPLOYMENT BEST PRACTICES

Best Practices for Deploying Node.js Real-Time Apps

When deploying Node.js real-time applications, such as chat apps, video streaming services, or collaborative tools, you must ensure that your app is highly available, scalable, and secure. Real-time apps often handle numerous concurrent connections, so optimizing deployment is crucial for performance and reliability.

Here are the key best practices for deploying real-time Node.js applications:

1. **Use Load Balancing:** Real-time apps handle multiple concurrent connections, and without proper load balancing, your server may become overwhelmed. **Load balancing** distributes incoming traffic across multiple servers to ensure that no single server gets overloaded, thus preventing bottlenecks.
   o Use **Nginx** or **HAProxy** as a reverse proxy to distribute WebSocket traffic across multiple backend servers.

224

- o **Horizontal scaling** is essential for real-time apps to handle growing numbers of connections.

2. **Optimize for Low Latency:** Real-time apps require low-latency communication between the client and the server. Optimizing your app's infrastructure for low latency includes:

   - o **Using a Content Delivery Network (CDN):** CDNs cache static content at edge locations close to users, reducing load times.

   - o **Geographically Distributed Servers:** Deploy your app across multiple data centers to minimize latency for users in different geographic regions.

3. **Monitor and Scale Automatically:** Real-time apps can have unpredictable spikes in traffic. Using **auto-scaling** ensures that your app can handle increased traffic by automatically provisioning additional instances during high-demand periods.

   - o **Cloud providers** like AWS, Azure, and Google Cloud offer auto-scaling groups that scale the number of instances up or down based on traffic volume.

   - o Implement monitoring tools such as **Prometheus**, **Grafana**, or **New Relic** to track application performance in real-time.

4. **Use WebSocket Connection Pools:** For applications relying on WebSockets, managing connections efficiently

is key. Pooling WebSocket connections ensures that the app doesn't exceed its connection limits, especially when scaling horizontally.

5. **Ensure High Availability:** High availability (HA) ensures that your application is resilient to failure. This can be achieved through:

   o **Database Replication:** Use master-slave or master-master replication to ensure that your database remains available even if one node goes down.

   o **Distributed Systems:** Use distributed systems (e.g., Redis, Kafka) to ensure that services remain available and consistent across multiple instances.

Using Docker for Containerization and Kubernetes for Orchestration

Containerization and orchestration are vital for deploying scalable and maintainable real-time applications. **Docker** and **Kubernetes** are two essential tools in modern cloud-native app deployment.

1. **Docker: Containerization for Consistency: Docker** allows you to package your Node.js real-time app and all its dependencies into a lightweight container. This

ensures that your app runs consistently across different environments, from local development to production.

- o **Dockerizing a Node.js App:**
  - Create a `Dockerfile` to specify how your app should be built and run inside the container.

Example Dockerfile:

```
dockerfile

# Use an official Node.js runtime as
a parent image
FROM node:14

# Set the working directory
WORKDIR /usr/src/app

#     package.json   and   install
dependencies
 package*.json ./
RUN npm install

# the rest of the app's source code
 . .

# Expose port 3000 for the app
EXPOSE 3000
```

```
# Start the app
CMD ["node", "app.js"]
```

- Build and run the Docker container:

```bash
docker build -t my-nodejs-app
.
docker run -p 3000:3000 my-nodejs-app
```

2. **Kubernetes: Orchestrating Containers for Scalability:** Kubernetes is an open-source container orchestration platform used to automate the deployment, scaling, and management of containerized applications. It is essential for deploying Node.js real-time apps at scale.

   o **Kubernetes Key Concepts:**

      - **Pods:** A pod is the smallest unit in Kubernetes, typically running a single container or a small group of containers that share resources.

      - **Services:** Kubernetes services enable communication between pods and expose your application to external traffic.

- **Ingress Controllers:** Ingress allows you to manage HTTP and HTTPS routing to your services in a Kubernetes cluster.
- **ReplicaSets:** These ensure that the desired number of replicas of a pod are running at any given time.

o **Setting Up Kubernetes Deployment:**

1. **Create a Deployment File** (`app-deployment.yaml`) to specify how many replicas of the app you want to run.

yaml

```yaml
apiVersion: apps/v1
kind: Deployment
metadata:
  name: my-nodejs-app
spec:
  replicas: 3
  selector:
    matchLabels:
      app: my-nodejs-app
  template:
    metadata:
      labels:
        app: my-nodejs-app
    spec:
      containers:
```

```
- name: my-nodejs-app
  image: my-nodejs-app:latest
  ports:
  - containerPort: 3000
```

- **Create a Service File** (app-service.yaml) to expose the app within the cluster or externally.

yaml

```yaml
apiVersion: v1
kind: Service
metadata:
  name: my-nodejs-app-service
spec:
  selector:
    app: my-nodejs-app
  ports:
    - protocol: TCP
      port: 80
      targetPort: 3000
  type: LoadBalancer
```

3. **Deploy to Kubernetes Cluster:** Use kubectl to apply the deployment and service files to your Kubernetes cluster.

bash

```
kubectl apply -f app-deployment.yaml
kubectl apply -f app-service.yaml
```

3. **Benefits of Using Kubernetes for Real-Time Apps:**

   o **Auto-scaling:** Kubernetes can automatically scale the number of pod replicas based on traffic or resource utilization.

   o **Rolling Updates:** Kubernetes allows for rolling updates of your application, minimizing downtime during updates.

   o **Self-Healing:** Kubernetes automatically restarts pods if they fail, ensuring high availability of the application.

Deployment Strategies for High-Availability Real-Time Apps

1. **Horizontal Scaling:** Horizontal scaling involves adding more instances of your real-time app to handle a growing number of concurrent users. Kubernetes, combined with Docker, allows you to easily scale the number of pods and handle a higher volume of traffic.

   o **Use Horizontal Pod Autoscaling (HPA):** Kubernetes can automatically scale your app based on CPU or memory usage.

Example HPA configuration:

yaml

```
apiVersion: autoscaling/v2
kind: HorizontalPodAutoscaler
metadata:
  name: my-nodejs-app-hpa
spec:
  scaleTargetRef:
    apiVersion: apps/v1
    kind: Deployment
    name: my-nodejs-app
  minReplicas: 2
  maxReplicas: 10
  metrics:
    - type: Resource
      resource:
        name: cpu
        target:
          type: Utilization
          averageUtilization: 50
```

2. **Load Balancing:** Load balancing is crucial for distributing traffic evenly across multiple instances of your application. Kubernetes provides built-in load balancing through services, and tools like **Nginx** can be used for more advanced routing.

o **Using Nginx for WebSocket Load Balancing:** Nginx can handle WebSocket connections and balance them across multiple Node.js instances. The configuration ensures that WebSocket connections are routed correctly.

nginx

```
http {
  upstream websocket {
    server nodejs-app-1:3000;
    server nodejs-app-2:3000;
  }

  server {
    listen 80;
    location / {
      proxy_pass http://websocket;
      proxy_http_version 1.1;
      proxy_set_header      Upgrade
$http_upgrade;
      proxy_set_header    Connection
'upgrade';
      proxy_set_header Host $host;
    }
  }
}
```

3. **Database Replication:** For high-availability real-time apps, database replication is critical to ensure data consistency across multiple nodes. Use **replica sets** for databases like MongoDB to ensure that read and write operations are distributed across multiple database nodes.

4. **Fault Tolerance and Redundancy:**
   o **Multiple Availability Zones:** Deploy your application across multiple availability zones (AZs) to prevent downtime if one AZ becomes unavailable.
   o **Backups and Disaster Recovery:** Implement a robust disaster recovery plan with regular backups of critical data.

Real-World Example: Deploying a Real-Time App on AWS with Docker and Kubernetes

Let's walk through the deployment of a **real-time chat app** using **Docker** and **Kubernetes** on **AWS**. This deployment will ensure high availability, scalability, and fault tolerance for your application.

1. **Set Up AWS EKS (Elastic Kubernetes Service):**
   o Use AWS EKS to create and manage a Kubernetes cluster.

- o Follow AWS documentation to create an EKS cluster using the AWS Management Console or `eksctl` CLI.

2. **Create Docker Containers for Your Real-Time App:**
   - o Dockerize your Node.js real-time app as shown earlier in this chapter.
   - o Push the Docker image to **Amazon Elastic Container Registry (ECR)**.

3. **Deploy on EKS:**
   - o Create a Kubernetes deployment and service files, as shown earlier.
   - o Apply the deployment using `kubectl` to deploy your app to EKS.

4. **Set Up Load Balancer:**
   - o Use AWS **Elastic Load Balancer (ELB)** to distribute traffic across multiple Node.js instances running in the EKS cluster.

5. **Monitor and Scale Automatically:**
   - o Set up **AWS CloudWatch** to monitor the performance and health of your app.
   - o Use **Horizontal Pod Autoscaler (HPA)** to automatically scale your app based on traffic and resource usage.

Conclusion

In this chapter, we covered the best practices for deploying **Node.js real-time apps** at scale, using **Docker** for containerization and **Kubernetes** for orchestration. We discussed how to ensure **high availability** through strategies like horizontal scaling, load balancing, and database replication.

We also walked through a **real-world example** of deploying a real-time app on **AWS** using Docker and Kubernetes. This setup ensures that your app is highly available, resilient to failures, and scalable to handle thousands or millions of concurrent users.

In the next chapters, we will continue to explore more advanced topics in deployment, including continuous integration/continuous deployment (CI/CD) pipelines, monitoring, and optimizing real-time apps in production.

CHAPTER 21

USING APIS AND WEBHOOKS FOR REAL-TIME INTERACTIONS

Introduction to APIs and Webhooks for Real-Time Integration

In modern web applications, **real-time interactions** are often achieved through the integration of **APIs** and **webhooks**. While both APIs and webhooks facilitate communication between different systems, they are used in different ways, and understanding when and how to use each can significantly enhance the functionality of your real-time application.

APIs are used to allow systems to request data from one another. A typical API call is a **client-initiated request** to a server, which returns the requested data. APIs are commonly used in real-time apps for operations like retrieving user data, sending messages, or updating a feed.

Webhooks, on the other hand, are used to allow a **server to send data to a client** in real time. They are typically used for **event-driven interactions**, where the server sends a notification to a client whenever a specific event occurs, such as a new order, a payment confirmation, or a new comment on a post.

Difference Between APIs and Webhooks:

- **APIs:** The client sends a request to the server to get data (client-initiated).
- **Webhooks:** The server sends data to the client automatically when an event happens (server-initiated).

Together, APIs and webhooks can be used to enable seamless real-time interactions between systems, making them essential tools in building modern, responsive applications.

Building and Consuming Webhooks in Node.js

In Node.js, **webhooks** can be implemented to handle event-driven communication, where external systems notify your app of certain actions or events. For example, you might want to integrate a payment gateway that sends a webhook whenever a payment is successfully completed.

Steps to Create and Handle Webhooks in Node.js:

1. **Set Up an Endpoint to Receive Webhooks:** First, you'll need to create an endpoint in your Node.js app that listens for incoming webhook requests. You can do this using Express.js, a lightweight Node.js web framework.

   ```
   javascript
   ```

```
const express = require('express');
const app = express();
const port = 3000;

// Middleware to parse incoming JSON body
app.use(express.json());

// Webhook endpoint to receive data
app.post('/webhook', (req, res) => {
  const payload = req.body;
  console.log('Received webhook payload:',
payload);

  // Process the webhook data (e.g., update
payment status)
  if           (payload.event          ===
'payment_received') {
    console.log('Payment          received.
Transaction ID:', payload.transaction_id);
  }

  // Respond with a success status
  res.status(200).send('Webhook
received');
});

app.listen(port, () => {
```

```
console.log(`Server     running     on
http://localhost:${port}`);
});
```

In this example:

- We set up a POST endpoint /webhook that listens for incoming webhook notifications.
- The body of the request (typically in JSON format) is parsed and processed based on the event type, such as "payment_received".
- After processing, the server responds with a success message (200 OK).

2. **Verify Webhook Signatures (Security):** Since webhooks are triggered by external systems, it's crucial to verify the authenticity of the incoming webhook requests. Many services (e.g., Stripe, PayPal) provide a **signature** in the request headers, which can be verified using a secret key.

Example of Verifying a Webhook Signature:

```javascript
const crypto = require('crypto');

const secret = 'your-webhook-secret'; // Secret key to verify the webhook
```

```javascript
app.post('/webhook', (req, res) => {
  const signature = req.headers['x-signature'];
  const payload = JSON.stringify(req.body);

  // Verify the signature
  const computedSignature = crypto
    .createHmac('sha256', secret)
    .update(payload)
    .digest('hex');

  if (computedSignature === signature) {
    console.log('Signature verified, processing webhook');
    // Handle webhook payload
  } else {
    console.error('Invalid signature');
    return res.status(400).send('Invalid signature');
  }

  res.status(200).send('Webhook received');
});
```

In this example:

- We compute a hash of the webhook payload using the secret key and compare it with the signature sent by the external system.
- If the signatures match, we proceed with processing the webhook; otherwise, we return an error.

3. **Sending Webhooks:** Webhooks are not limited to just receiving data. You can also use webhooks to **send data to other systems** whenever certain events occur in your application. This is useful when you want to notify an external system about a change, such as a new user registration, a payment update, or an item purchase.

Example of Sending a Webhook:

```javascript
const axios = require('axios');

function sendWebhook(eventData) {
  axios.post('https://external-
system.com/webhook', eventData)
    .then(response => {
      console.log('Webhook                sent
successfully:', response.data);
    })
    .catch(error => {
```

```
        console.error('Error          sending
webhook:', error);
    });
}


// Example usage: send a webhook when a new
payment is completed
const paymentData = {
  event: 'payment_received',
  transaction_id: '12345',
  amount: 100,
};


sendWebhook(paymentData);
```

In this example:

- o We use **axios**, a promise-based HTTP client, to send a `POST` request to an external system whenever a specific event occurs.
- o The data (payload) is sent in the request body.

Real-World Example: Integrating a Payment Gateway with Webhooks for Real-Time Transactions

Let's implement a real-world example of using **webhooks** to integrate a payment gateway for real-time payment notifications.

In this example, we'll use **Stripe** as the payment gateway, which sends a webhook when a payment is successfully processed.

Step 1: Set Up Webhook Listener for Payment Confirmation

1. **Create a Webhook Endpoint to Receive Stripe Events:**

   When a payment is made using Stripe, Stripe will send a webhook to your server containing information about the transaction.

   javascript

```javascript
const express = require('express');
const bodyParser = require('body-parser');
const stripe = require('stripe')('your-
stripe-secret-key');  // Stripe secret key
const app = express();

// Middleware to parse incoming JSON body
app.use(bodyParser.raw({              type:
'application/json' }));

app.post('/webhook', (req, res) => {
  const sig    =    req.headers['stripe-
signature'];
  const payload = req.body;

  let event;
```

```
try {
  // Verify the webhook signature
  event                                    =
stripe.webhooks.constructEvent(payload,
sig, 'your-webhook-secret');
  } catch (err) {
    console.error('Error verifying webhook
signature:', err.message);
    return    res.status(400).send(`Webhook
error: ${err.message}`);
  }


  // Handle the event
  if              (event.type              ===
'payment_intent.succeeded') {
    const          paymentIntent          =
event.data.object;
    console.log(`PaymentIntent          for
${paymentIntent.amount} was successful!`);
    // Process the successful payment
(e.g., mark the order as paid)
  } else {
    console.log('Unhandled  event  type:',
event.type);
  }


  res.status(200).send('Webhook
received');
```

```
});

app.listen(3000, () => {
  console.log('Server          running          on
http://localhost:3000');
});
```

Explanation:

- o We use the
  `stripe.webhooks.constructEvent()`
  method to verify the webhook signature from
  Stripe. This ensures that the request came from
  Stripe and wasn't tampered with.
- o We handle the `payment_intent.succeeded`
  event, which is triggered when a payment is
  successfully processed. The payment details are
  available in the event data, allowing you to update
  your order status, send confirmation emails, or
  trigger any other actions.

Step 2: Test the Webhook with Stripe:

Stripe allows you to test webhooks using the Stripe Dashboard or
Stripe CLI. You can simulate events (e.g.,
`payment_intent.succeeded`) and send them to your server
for testing.

1. **Install Stripe CLI:**

bash

```
npm install -g stripe-cli
```

2. **Forward Events to Your Local Server:**

bash

```
stripe listen --forward-to
localhost:3000/webhook
```

3. **Trigger a Test Event:** In the Stripe Dashboard or using the CLI, you can trigger a test payment that will automatically send a webhook to your server.

Conclusion

In this chapter, we explored how to use **APIs and webhooks** to integrate real-time interactions in your application. We covered the following topics:

- **Building and Consuming Webhooks:** We discussed how to set up webhook listeners and send webhooks in Node.js. Webhooks are essential for real-time, event-driven interactions, allowing your application to respond to external events (e.g., payment confirmation, system updates).

- **Securing Webhooks:** We covered how to verify the authenticity of incoming webhooks using signatures to ensure that requests come from trusted sources.

- **Real-World Example:** We integrated a **payment gateway** (Stripe) into a Node.js app, using webhooks to handle real-time payment notifications and process them accordingly.

Webhooks are powerful tools for integrating real-time services and building responsive, event-driven applications. In the next chapters, we will dive deeper into advanced webhook handling, scaling, and monitoring strategies to ensure the reliability and efficiency of your real-time apps.

CHAPTER 22

MANAGING REAL-TIME EVENTS AND QUEUES

Event-Driven Architecture in Node.js

Event-driven architecture (EDA) is a design pattern where the flow of the program is driven by events—changes in state or specific actions that occur in real time. This architecture is ideal for real-time applications, as it allows the system to respond dynamically to different inputs or events as they occur, rather than relying on a static, predefined sequence of operations.

In Node.js, event-driven architecture is a natural fit due to its asynchronous, non-blocking I/O model. Node.js operates around the concept of the **event loop**, where events are captured and processed by handlers (callbacks). This enables it to handle a large number of I/O-bound tasks concurrently without blocking the main thread, making it particularly effective for real-time applications that require high responsiveness.

Key Components of Event-Driven Architecture:

1. **Events:** Represent actions or changes in state (e.g., new message, new order, new user login).

2. **Event Emitters:** In Node.js, the `EventEmitter` class (part of the `events` module) is used to create and handle events.

3. **Event Handlers (Listeners):** Functions that listen for specific events and perform actions when the event occurs.

Event-Driven Architecture in Node.js Example:

javascript

```javascript
const EventEmitter = require('events');
const orderEmitter = new EventEmitter();

// Event listener for new order
orderEmitter.on('newOrder', (order) => {
  console.log(`Processing order ${order.id}`);
  // Process the order
});

// Simulating a new order
orderEmitter.emit('newOrder',   {   id:   123,
product: 'Laptop' });
```

In this example:

- We use an `EventEmitter` to emit a `newOrder` event when a new order is placed.
- An event listener is triggered to handle the event and process the order.

This simple event-driven model is scalable and can be expanded to manage various events, such as user registration, payment processing, and notifications.

Using Message Queues Like RabbitMQ or Kafka for Real-Time Events

Message queues are essential tools for managing real-time events and asynchronous communication in distributed systems. They enable applications to **decouple components**, ensuring that each service or component can operate independently without directly relying on others. Message queues are particularly useful when you need to process events in real-time but at different rates or with different priorities.

Message Queues Overview:

- **RabbitMQ:** A widely-used message broker that supports AMQP (Advanced Message Queuing Protocol). RabbitMQ is great for scenarios where you need reliability, high-throughput, and flexible routing of messages.

- **Kafka:** A distributed event streaming platform that is designed for handling large-scale, real-time data feeds. Kafka is highly scalable and can handle high-throughput, fault-tolerant event processing across many services.

Both RabbitMQ and Kafka allow real-time applications to handle events such as user actions, transactions, and notifications asynchronously, ensuring that each event is processed in a way that doesn't block the main workflow of the application.

Why Use Message Queues for Real-Time Events?

1. **Asynchronous Processing:** Queues decouple event producers (e.g., a user placing an order) from event consumers (e.g., processing payment or shipping), allowing each service to process events at its own pace.
2. **Reliability:** Queues ensure that messages are not lost. If a consumer service is unavailable, messages are retained in the queue until the service is available again.
3. **Scalability:** With Kafka, for example, you can scale event processing horizontally by adding more consumers as traffic grows.

Example: Implementing RabbitMQ for Real-Time Events in Node.js

1. **Install the Required Dependencies:** You need the `amqplib` package to interact with RabbitMQ from Node.js.

```bash
bash
```

```bash
npm install amqplib
```

2. **Set Up the RabbitMQ Publisher:** This part of the application sends messages (events) to the queue.

```javascript
javascript

const amqp = require('amqplib');

async function sendToQueue() {
  const connection = await amqp.connect('amqp://localhost');
  const channel = await connection.createChannel();
  const queue = 'orderQueue';

  // Assert the queue exists
  await channel.assertQueue(queue, { durable: true });

  // Send a message to the queue
  const order = { id: 123, product: 'Laptop' };
```

```
  channel.sendToQueue(queue,
Buffer.from(JSON.stringify(order)),          {
persistent: true });
  console.log('Sent order:', order);

  setTimeout(() => {
    connection.close();
  }, 500);
}

sendToQueue();
```

3. **Set Up the RabbitMQ Consumer:** This part listens for messages from the queue and processes them when they arrive.

javascript

```
const amqp = require('amqplib');

async function consumeFromQueue() {
  const        connection        =        await
amqp.connect('amqp://localhost');
  const        channel        =        await
connection.createChannel();
  const queue = 'orderQueue';

  // Assert the queue exists
```

```
  await    channel.assertQueue(queue,    {
durable: true });

  // Set up a consumer to process orders
  console.log('Waiting for orders...');
  channel.consume(queue, (msg) => {
    const         order         =
JSON.parse(msg.content.toString());
    console.log('Processing    order:',
order);
    channel.ack(msg); // Acknowledge the
message has been processed
  }, { noAck: false });
}

consumeFromQueue();
```

Explanation:

- The **publisher** sends an order message to the orderQueue, which is stored until the consumer processes it.
- The **consumer** waits for messages and processes them as they arrive, handling each order individually.

This simple RabbitMQ-based example can be scaled out with additional services that consume messages from the queue and process them in parallel, allowing for efficient and reliable handling of real-time events in a distributed system.

Real-World Example: Processing Real-Time Orders in an E-Commerce App

Let's build a real-world scenario where an **e-commerce platform** processes **real-time orders** using message queues (e.g., RabbitMQ) for asynchronous processing. In this example, we'll simulate processing an order with real-time updates.

Step 1: Place an Order (Publish the Event) When a user places an order on the e-commerce platform, an event is triggered, and the order is published to the message queue (RabbitMQ). This event may include details such as the items ordered, customer information, and payment status.

Publisher (Order Service):

javascript

```javascript
const amqp = require('amqplib');

async function publishOrder(order) {
    const connection = await amqp.connect('amqp://localhost');
    const channel = await connection.createChannel();
    const queue = 'orderQueue';
```

```javascript
  await channel.assertQueue(queue, { durable:
true });
  channel.sendToQueue(queue,
Buffer.from(JSON.stringify(order)),              {
persistent: true });

  console.log('Order placed:', order);

  setTimeout(() => {
    connection.close();
  }, 500);
}


const order = { id: 12345, product: 'Laptop',
customer: 'John Doe', status: 'Pending' };
publishOrder(order);
```

Step 2: Process the Order (Consume the Event) Once the order is placed, the **payment service** (or another backend service) consumes the message and processes the payment.

Consumer (Payment Service):

javascript

```javascript
const amqp = require('amqplib');

async function processOrder() {
  const       connection       =       await
amqp.connect('amqp://localhost');
```

```javascript
  const          channel          =          await
connection.createChannel();
  const queue = 'orderQueue';

  await  channel.assertQueue(queue,  {  durable:
true });
  console.log('Waiting for orders...');

  channel.consume(queue, async (msg) => {
    const              order              =
JSON.parse(msg.content.toString());
    console.log('Processing order:', order);
    await processPayment(order);
    channel.ack(msg); // Acknowledge the message
as processed
  }, { noAck: false });
}

async function processPayment(order) {
  console.log(`Processing  payment  for  order
${order.id}`);
  // Simulate a delay in processing the payment
  setTimeout(() => {
    console.log(`Payment  successful  for  order
${order.id}`);
    // After payment, send a success message or
proceed with shipping
  }, 3000);
}
```

```
processOrder();
```

Explanation:

1. When a user places an order, the **Order Service** publishes an event to RabbitMQ (`orderQueue`).

2. The **Payment Service** consumes the event, processes the payment asynchronously, and then acknowledges that the order has been processed.

3. Once the payment is processed, other services (e.g., Shipping, Notification) can consume the order and proceed with their tasks.

This real-time, event-driven approach allows the system to process multiple orders concurrently, scale as needed, and handle failures more effectively by decoupling the different services.

Conclusion

In this chapter, we explored the concept of **event-driven architecture** in real-time applications and how to implement it in **Node.js** using message queues like **RabbitMQ** and **Kafka**. We covered:

- The basics of **event-driven architecture** and how to use event emitters in Node.js.
- **Message queues** and how they can be used for processing real-time events asynchronously and reliably.
- A **real-world example** of processing **real-time orders** in an e-commerce app using RabbitMQ.

By implementing message queues in your real-time applications, you can decouple services, handle high volumes of events, and improve the scalability and resilience of your systems. In the next chapters, we will dive deeper into advanced event processing techniques and scaling strategies for real-time applications.

CHAPTER 23

REAL-TIME ANALYTICS AND MONITORING

The Need for Real-Time Analytics in Modern Web Apps

In modern web applications, understanding user behavior, system performance, and real-time data trends is crucial for making informed decisions. **Real-time analytics** allows businesses to track key metrics and make instant adjustments to improve user experience, optimize system performance, and respond to emerging trends or issues.

Real-time analytics can be particularly useful in scenarios such as:

- **E-commerce platforms:** Tracking live inventory, sales, and customer behavior to optimize product recommendations and pricing strategies.
- **Social media apps:** Monitoring live user interactions (e.g., likes, shares, comments) to ensure engagement and detect patterns.
- **Gaming platforms:** Real-time monitoring of in-game activity, player behavior, and game performance to provide instant feedback and updates.

The need for real-time analytics comes from the desire to make **instant decisions** based on the most current data available. For example, an e-commerce site might want to instantly display offers to users based on their activity or provide real-time feedback on a user's actions.

Real-time analytics also plays a significant role in **monitoring system health,** tracking error rates, performance bottlenecks, and ensuring that the app continues to provide a seamless experience to its users.

Setting Up Real-Time Monitoring Dashboards

A **real-time monitoring dashboard** provides a central location for viewing key metrics and system health in real-time. Dashboards allow stakeholders, system administrators, and developers to monitor performance, detect issues, and take immediate action if needed.

Steps to Set Up Real-Time Monitoring Dashboards:

1. **Choose a Monitoring Tool:** Several tools provide real-time analytics and dashboards. Some popular options include:

   o **Grafana:** Open-source software that integrates with various data sources, such as Prometheus,

InfluxDB, and Elasticsearch, to provide real-time visualizations.

- o **Kibana:** A visualization tool that works with Elasticsearch, often used for real-time log and event monitoring.
- o **Datadog:** A cloud-based monitoring and analytics platform that provides real-time data monitoring, alerting, and visualization.
- o **Prometheus:** A time-series database and monitoring system that integrates well with Grafana for real-time visualizations.

2. **Integrating Real-Time Data Sources:** To display real-time data on the dashboard, you need to continuously feed data into the monitoring system. In Node.js, you can use libraries like **Socket.IO**, **WebSocket**, or **REST APIs** to push data to the dashboard.

3. **Create Real-Time Metrics:** Define the metrics you want to monitor in real-time. Common metrics for web apps include:

- o **User activity metrics:** Page views, clicks, user sessions, and interactions.
- o **Performance metrics:** Response time, CPU usage, memory usage, and database queries.
- o **Business metrics:** Sales, conversion rates, inventory levels, and customer interactions.

4. **Visualize Metrics:** Once you have the data, use visualization tools like Grafana to display the data in real-time. Grafana allows you to create real-time dashboards with charts, graphs, tables, and alerts.

Example of Setting Up Grafana with Prometheus for Real-Time Metrics:

- o Install Prometheus to collect time-series data from your Node.js app.
- o Install Grafana and configure it to pull data from Prometheus.
- o Use Grafana to create dashboards that display live metrics, such as the number of active users, response times, and system health.

5. **Alerting:** Set up alerts to notify you when certain metrics reach predefined thresholds. For example, you can set up alerts to trigger when response times exceed a certain limit or if CPU usage becomes too high.

Real-Time Data Analytics with Node.js

Node.js, with its non-blocking I/O model, is a great fit for real-time data processing. Whether you need to process real-time logs, track user activities, or analyze live data streams, Node.js can handle these tasks efficiently.

Steps to Implement Real-Time Analytics with Node.js:

1. **Collect Real-Time Data:**
    o   Use event-driven architecture to collect real-time events from users or systems. For instance, you can use **WebSockets** to track live user activity or **message queues** (e.g., RabbitMQ or Kafka) to consume real-time events.

    Example of Collecting User Activity via WebSockets:

    javascript

    ```javascript
    const WebSocket = require('ws');
    const wss = new WebSocket.Server({ port:
    8080 });

    wss.on('connection', (ws) => {
      console.log('User connected');

      ws.on('message', (data) => {
        console.log('User activity:', data);
        // Save or process the activity data
    for analytics
      });
    });
    ```

2. **Store Data for Real-Time Analytics:** Store the incoming data in a time-series database like **InfluxDB** or use a

NoSQL database like **MongoDB** to store and query the data efficiently.

3. **Process and Aggregate Data:**
   o For real-time analytics, you need to aggregate the data efficiently. You can use libraries like **Lodash** or **Underscore** in Node.js for aggregating and transforming data.
   o For advanced processing, consider using a stream-processing system such as **Apache Kafka Streams** or **Apache Flink**.

4. **Push Processed Data to a Dashboard:** Once the data is processed, send it to the dashboard using WebSockets or HTTP APIs.

Example of Sending Processed Data to Grafana via Prometheus:

javascript

```
const prometheus = require('prom-client');
const       register      =       new
prometheus.Registry();

// Define metrics
const activeUsers = new prometheus.Gauge({
  name: 'active_users',
  help: 'Number of active users',
});
```

266

```
// Update active users
setInterval(() => {

activeUsers.set(Math.floor(Math.random() *
100)); // Example data
}, 1000);

// Expose metrics to Prometheus
app.get('/metrics', (req, res) => {
  res.set('Content-Type',
register.contentType);
  res.end(register.metrics());
});
```

5. **Real-Time Querying and Visualization:** Use Grafana or another visualization tool to visualize the real-time data on a dashboard. You can create custom graphs to display metrics like active users, order counts, and website traffic.

Real-World Example: Tracking Live User Activity on a Website

Let's consider an e-commerce website where we want to track user activity in real time. We want to capture when users log in, add items to their cart, and make purchases. This information can be used for real-time analytics, such as personalized recommendations or tracking product popularity.

Step 1: Collecting User Activity Data

We'll use **WebSockets** to collect real-time user activity data and send it to a backend service for processing.

Client-Side (Tracking User Activity):

html

```html
<!DOCTYPE html>
<html lang="en">
<head>
  <meta charset="UTF-8">
  <meta name="viewport" content="width=device-width, initial-scale=1.0">
  <title>User Activity Tracker</title>
</head>
<body>
  <h1>E-Commerce Website</h1>
  <button id="add-to-cart">Add to Cart</button>

  <script>
    const ws = new WebSocket('wss://your-server.com');

    document.getElementById('add-to-cart').addEventListener('click', () => {
      const activityData = {
        event: 'add-to-cart',
        userId: 'user123',
```

```
    productId: 'product567',
    timestamp: new Date().toISOString(),
  };

  ws.send(JSON.stringify(activityData)); //
Send activity to WebSocket server
  });
  </script>
</body>
</html>
```

Step 2: Receiving and Storing User Activity (Node.js Server)

On the server, we will listen for WebSocket messages and store the user activity in a database.

Server-Side (Node.js):

javascript

```
const WebSocket = require('ws');
const mongoose = require('mongoose');

// Connect to MongoDB (or use a database of your
choice)
mongoose.connect('mongodb://localhost:27017/use
rActivity',      {      useNewUrlParser:      true,
useUnifiedTopology: true });

// Define the schema and model
const activitySchema = new mongoose.Schema({
```

```
  event: String,
  userId: String,
  productId: String,
  timestamp: Date,
});
const  Activity  =  mongoose.model('Activity',
activitySchema);

const wss = new WebSocket.Server({ port: 8080 });

wss.on('connection', (ws) => {
  ws.on('message', async (data) => {
    const activity = JSON.parse(data);
    console.log('User Activity:', activity);

    // Save activity to database
    const newActivity = new Activity(activity);
    await newActivity.save();
  });
});
```

Step 3: Setting Up Real-Time Dashboard with Grafana

Now that we have real-time user activity data, we can expose this data to Grafana for real-time visualization.

1. Install **Prometheus** to collect metrics and expose them to Grafana.

2. Use Prometheus to scrape data from your Node.js app using a custom `/metrics` endpoint.

3. Set up **Grafana** to create dashboards that display metrics such as:

   o Number of active users

   o Products added to cart

   o Purchase conversion rates

Conclusion

In this chapter, we explored **real-time analytics and monitoring** for web apps, focusing on how to collect, process, and visualize data in real time. We covered the importance of tracking user behavior, system performance, and other key metrics using real-time dashboards.

We learned how to:

- Implement **real-time user activity tracking** using WebSockets.
- Use **Prometheus** to expose metrics and visualize them using **Grafana**.
- Integrate **real-time analytics** with Node.js to gain insights into user interactions on your website.

Real-time analytics and monitoring help you stay ahead of issues, optimize user experience, and make informed decisions in real-time. In the next chapters, we will continue to explore advanced monitoring techniques and best practices for scaling and optimizing real-time systems.

CHAPTER 24

REAL-TIME SECURITY CHALLENGES AND SOLUTIONS

Security Concerns in Real-Time Web Apps

Real-time web applications are essential for providing live interactions, like chat services, video streaming, and gaming. However, these applications also introduce several unique **security concerns** due to the constant, bidirectional communication between clients and servers. Real-time interactions, such as WebSocket connections or API calls for live data, must be secured to prevent various types of attacks and data breaches.

Key Security Concerns in Real-Time Web Apps:

1. **Unauthorized Access:** Real-time applications often need to manage user sessions and sensitive data, making unauthorized access a major risk.

2. **Data Privacy:** Real-time communication systems, especially those involving messaging or financial transactions, may be vulnerable to data interception and leakage.

3. **Man-in-the-Middle (MITM) Attacks:** In insecure communication channels, attackers could intercept or alter data being exchanged between clients and servers.

4. **Denial of Service (DoS) and Distributed Denial of Service (DDoS) Attacks:** Real-time apps with many simultaneous connections are prime targets for DoS/DDoS attacks, which flood the server with excessive traffic to make it unresponsive.

5. **Replay Attacks:** Attackers may intercept valid requests and replay them to carry out unauthorized actions.

6. **Session Hijacking:** Real-time apps must manage active sessions and prevent attackers from taking control of a user's session.

Real-time apps must implement robust security measures to mitigate these concerns. Protecting user data, ensuring secure communication, and preventing various types of attacks are critical steps in developing secure real-time applications.

Protecting Against DoS and DDoS Attacks

Denial of Service (DoS) and Distributed Denial of Service (DDoS) attacks aim to overwhelm your application or server, causing it to crash or become unresponsive. This can be a significant threat to real-time applications that rely on live data and continuous client-server communication.

DoS and DDoS Attack Mitigation Strategies:

1. **Rate Limiting:** Implement **rate limiting** to restrict the number of requests a user or IP can make in a given period. This can help prevent flood attacks from overwhelming your server.

   o **Example of Rate Limiting with Express.js:**

   javascript

   ```javascript
   const rateLimit = require('express-rate-limit');

   const limiter = rateLimit({
     windowMs: 15 * 60 * 1000, // 15 minutes
     max: 100, // Limit each IP to 100 requests per windowMs
     message: 'Too many requests, please try again later.'
   });

   app.use(limiter);
   ```

2. **Web Application Firewall (WAF):** Use a WAF to block traffic from malicious sources. A WAF can filter out suspicious traffic patterns before they reach your application servers.

  o Services like **Cloudflare** or **AWS WAF** can help protect against DDoS attacks by filtering out traffic that looks like a DDoS attack.

3. **Traffic Monitoring:** Implement **real-time traffic monitoring** to detect unusual spikes in traffic. Tools like **Prometheus** and **Grafana** can be used to track the number of incoming requests and alert you when thresholds are exceeded.

4. **Load Balancing and Auto-Scaling:** Use **load balancers** to distribute incoming traffic across multiple instances of your application. In the event of high traffic, **auto-scaling** ensures that new instances of your app are created dynamically to handle the load.

5. **Reverse Proxies and CDN Protection:** Implement a **reverse proxy** (e.g., Nginx) and use a **Content Delivery Network (CDN),** such as **Cloudflare**, to filter out malicious traffic before it reaches your application. CDNs can absorb DDoS attacks by caching content at edge locations and serving it from multiple servers.

Securing WebSocket Connections and Data

WebSocket connections are a core component of real-time web applications, allowing for continuous bidirectional communication between the client and server. However, these connections must be properly secured to prevent unauthorized access, data tampering, and eavesdropping.

WebSocket Security Best Practices:

1. **Use Secure WebSocket Protocol (WSS):** Always use **WSS** (WebSocket Secure) instead of **WS**. WSS encrypts the data transmitted over the WebSocket connection using **SSL/TLS**, ensuring that sensitive information is protected from man-in-the-middle attacks.

   Example of WSS:

   ```javascript
   const WebSocket = require('ws');
   const server = new WebSocket.Server({
     port: 8080,
     secure: true, // Enforce secure WebSocket
   (WSS)
     ssl: {
       cert:
   fs.readFileSync('path/to/certificate.pem'
   ),
       key: fs.readFileSync('path/to/private-
   key.pem'),
     }
   });
   ```

2. **Authenticate WebSocket Connections:** Use **JWT (JSON Web Tokens)** or another authentication method to ensure that only authorized users can establish WebSocket connections. This can be done by verifying the token during the WebSocket handshake.

Example of JWT Authentication in WebSocket:

```javascript
javascript

const WebSocket = require('ws');
const jwt = require('jsonwebtoken');

const wss = new WebSocket.Server({ port: 8080 });

wss.on('connection', (ws, req) => {
  const token = req.headers['authorization']?.split(' ')[1]; // Extract JWT from the header

  if (!token) {
    ws.close(); // Close the connection if no token is provided
    return;
  }

  jwt.verify(token, 'secret-key', (err, decoded) => {
```

```
if (err) {
    ws.close(); // Close connection if
JWT is invalid
    return;
}

    console.log('Authenticated     user:',
decoded.username);
  });

  ws.on('message', (message) => {
    console.log('Received        message:',
message);
  });
});
```

3. **Use Message Encryption for Sensitive Data:** Even if your WebSocket connection is secure (WSS), you may want to **encrypt the actual messages** sent between the client and server, especially for sensitive data like financial transactions or personal information. This ensures that if someone intercepts the WebSocket traffic, they cannot read the contents of the messages.

Example of Encrypting WebSocket Messages:

```javascript
javascript

const crypto = require('crypto');
```

```
const algorithm = 'aes-256-ctr';
const password = 'password';   // Use a
secure key

function encryptMessage(message) {
  const             cipher             =
crypto.createCipher(algorithm, password);
  let encrypted = cipher.update(message,
'utf8', 'hex');
  encrypted += cipher.final('hex');
  return encrypted;
}


function  decryptMessage(encryptedMessage)
{
  const            decipher            =
crypto.createDecipher(algorithm,
password);
  let             decrypted             =
decipher.update(encryptedMessage,   'hex',
'utf8');
  decrypted += decipher.final('utf8');
  return decrypted;
}
```

4. **Implement Rate Limiting and Connection Throttling:** WebSocket servers can be vulnerable to abuse, such as excessive connections or too many messages being sent in a short time. Implement **rate limiting** and **connection**

throttling to prevent users from overwhelming your WebSocket server.

- o Limit the number of WebSocket connections from a single IP address.
- o Use message queueing systems (e.g., RabbitMQ or Kafka) to throttle the flow of messages between clients and servers, preventing spamming.

Real-World Example: Building a Secure Real-Time Application for Financial Services

Let's consider building a **real-time financial services application** that securely handles real-time transactions and account updates. The application requires secure communication between clients and the server, including encrypted data transmission and authentication.

Step 1: Secure WebSocket Connections (WSS)

Use **WSS** to ensure that all WebSocket connections are encrypted and secure.

javascript

```javascript
const WebSocket = require('ws');
const fs = require('fs');
```

```javascript
const wss = new WebSocket.Server({
  port: 8080,
  secure: true, // Enforce secure WebSocket (WSS)
  ssl: {
    cert:
fs.readFileSync('path/to/certificate.pem'),
    key:        fs.readFileSync('path/to/private-
key.pem'),
  }
});

wss.on('connection', (ws) => {
  console.log('Client connected securely');
  ws.on('message', (message) => {
    console.log('Received message:', message);
  });
});
```

Step 2: Authenticate WebSocket Connections with JWT

Ensure that users are authenticated before they can participate in the transaction process.

```
javascript
```

```javascript
const jwt = require('jsonwebtoken');

wss.on('connection', (ws, req) => {
```

```javascript
const                    token                    =
req.headers['authorization']?.split(' ')[1];

  if (!token) {
    ws.close();
    return;
  }

  jwt.verify(token,      'your-secure-secret-key',
(err, decoded) => {
    if (err) {
      ws.close();
      return;
    }

    console.log('Authenticated            user:',
decoded.username);
  });
});
```

Step 3: Process Real-Time Transactions and Handle Security

In this step, when a user initiates a transaction, it is encrypted and sent through the WebSocket. Only authorized and authenticated users are allowed to proceed.

```javascript
javascript

function processTransaction(transactionData) {
  // Simulate transaction processing
```

```javascript
  console.log(`Processing     transaction     for
account: ${transactionData.accountId}`);
  // Further  transaction  logic  here  (e.g.,
debit/credit accounts)
}


// Handle real-time transaction
wss.on('connection', (ws) => {
  ws.on('message', (message) => {
    const           decryptedMessage          =
decryptMessage(message);
    const            transactionData           =
JSON.parse(decryptedMessage);

    if (transactionData.type === 'transfer') {
      processTransaction(transactionData);
    }
  });
});
```

Step 4: Encrypt Transaction Data for Added Security

Encrypt sensitive transaction data before sending it through the WebSocket connection to ensure confidentiality.

```
javascript
```

```javascript
function encryptMessage(message) {
  const cipher = crypto.createCipher(algorithm,
password);
```

```
let encrypted = cipher.update(message, 'utf8',
'hex');
encrypted += cipher.final('hex');
return encrypted;
}
```

Conclusion

In this chapter, we discussed the security challenges in **real-time web applications** and provided solutions for securing WebSocket connections, protecting against DoS/DDoS attacks, and ensuring data privacy. We also covered:

- **Securing WebSocket connections** with **WSS** and **JWT authentication** to ensure that only authorized users can access sensitive data.
- **Encrypting data** transmitted over WebSockets to protect transaction information.
- Implementing security strategies to safeguard real-time applications against **DDoS attacks, session hijacking**, and other security risks.

The real-world example showed how to build a **secure real-time application for financial services**, processing transactions in real time with encryption, authentication, and secure WebSocket connections.

In the next chapters, we will dive deeper into additional security strategies, including multi-factor authentication (MFA), advanced encryption techniques, and securing APIs and data at rest in real-time systems.

CHAPTER 25

HANDLING MOBILE REAL-TIME APPLICATIONS

Challenges of Building Real-Time Mobile Applications

Building real-time mobile applications comes with unique challenges due to the constraints of mobile devices, the need for low-latency interactions, and the complexities of network connectivity. Here are some of the most common challenges:

1. **Network Connectivity:**
   - o **Mobile networks** can be unstable, especially on cellular networks where users may experience fluctuations in connection speed or dropouts.
   - o Real-time apps need to handle situations where the network is intermittent or slow, ensuring a consistent experience even with unreliable network conditions.

2. **Latency:**
   - o Mobile devices often have higher **latency** compared to desktop applications due to network distance and limited processing power.

o To ensure smooth real-time interactions, minimizing latency is essential, which requires efficient use of communication protocols and network optimization.

3. **Battery Life:**

   o Real-time applications that require constant background communication, such as messaging apps or notifications, can drain battery life quickly.

   o Efficient management of resources and background tasks is crucial for keeping the app responsive without negatively affecting the device's battery life.

4. **Scaling to Millions of Users:**

   o Mobile real-time apps must scale efficiently to handle large numbers of concurrent users, particularly in applications like social media or messaging platforms.

   o Handling the **data synchronization** and ensuring that updates happen quickly and reliably can be complex when there are millions of active users.

5. **Handling Data Synchronization:**

   o In real-time mobile apps, data synchronization between the server and client must be handled efficiently to ensure that the client gets live updates without unnecessarily overloading the server.

o **Conflicts** can arise when users are editing the same data or making changes in a disconnected state.

Using Node.js for Real-Time Mobile Backends

Node.js is a great choice for building backends for real-time mobile applications due to its **non-blocking, event-driven architecture**. It can efficiently handle thousands of concurrent connections, making it perfect for real-time data streaming, messaging, and notifications. Here's how you can use Node.js for real-time mobile backends:

1. **Handling WebSocket Connections:** WebSockets allow you to establish persistent, low-latency connections between the mobile client and server. With **Socket.IO** or **native WebSockets**, Node.js can facilitate real-time bi-directional communication between clients (mobile apps) and the server.

   Example: Setting Up a WebSocket Server in Node.js:

   ```javascript
   const express = require('express');
   ```

```javascript
const http = require('http');
const socketIo = require('socket.io');

const app = express();
const server = http.createServer(app);
const io = socketIo(server);

io.on('connection', (socket) => {
  console.log('A user connected');
  socket.on('disconnect', () => {
    console.log('A user disconnected');
  });

  // Emit a message to the client
  socket.emit('message', 'Hello, Mobile Client!');
});

server.listen(3000, () => {
  console.log('Server is running on http://localhost:3000');
});
```

2. **Real-Time Messaging:** In real-time mobile apps like **messaging apps**, each message needs to be transmitted instantly. Using **Socket.IO** with Node.js allows bi-directional communication to transmit messages between mobile clients in real time.

290

3. **Push Notifications:** In addition to WebSockets, **push notifications** are commonly used in mobile apps to notify users of real-time events, even when they are not actively using the app. Services like **Firebase Cloud Messaging (FCM)** or **Apple Push Notification Service (APNS)** can be integrated with Node.js to send notifications.

Example: Sending Push Notifications with Firebase Cloud Messaging (FCM):

```javascript
const admin = require('firebase-admin');

// Initialize Firebase Admin SDK
admin.initializeApp({
  credential:
admin.credential.cert('path/to/serviceAcc
ountKey.json')
});

// Send a push notification to a specific
device
const message = {
  token: 'device_token',
  notification: {
    title: 'New Message',
    body: 'You have a new message!',
  },
```

291

```
};

admin.messaging().send(message)
  .then(response => {
    console.log('Notification        sent
successfully:', response);
  })
  .catch(error => {
    console.log('Error        sending
notification:', error);
  });
```

4. **Database Integration:** Node.js can easily integrate with databases like **MongoDB** or **PostgreSQL** to store and retrieve real-time data. For instance, in messaging apps, **MongoDB** can be used to store user messages and retrieve them as needed, while **Redis** can be used for session management and caching.

Integrating Real-Time Features with Mobile Apps

Integrating real-time features in a mobile app involves setting up both the server-side and client-side components. Here's how you can integrate real-time capabilities into your mobile apps:

1. **Setting Up WebSocket on the Client Side (React Native Example):** React Native allows you to build

cross-platform mobile applications, and integrating real-time features like WebSockets is straightforward.

Example: React Native WebSocket Client for Real-Time Messaging:

javascript

```
import React, { useEffect, useState } from
'react';
import { View, Text, Button } from 'react-native';

const App = () => {
  const [message, setMessage] =
useState('');

  useEffect(() => {
    const socket = new
WebSocket('ws://localhost:3000');

    socket.onopen = () => {
      console.log('WebSocket connected');
    };

    socket.onmessage = (event) => {
      setMessage(event.data);    //    Set
received message to state
    };
```

```
socket.onclose = () => {
  console.log('WebSocket closed');
};

return () => {
  socket.close();
};
}, []);

return (
  <View>
    <Text>{message}</Text>
    <Button    title="Send    Message"
onPress={() => {
      const    socket    =    new
WebSocket('ws://localhost:3000');
      socket.send('Hello from mobile!');
    }} />
  </View>
);
};


export default App;
```

2. **Handling Real-Time Notifications:** To handle real-time notifications, integrate a push notification service like **FCM** or **APNS** into your mobile app. These services

enable you to send notifications even when the app is not open.

- o Use the **Firebase SDK** in your mobile app to subscribe for push notifications and handle them accordingly.

Example of Push Notification Integration in React Native:

```javascript
import messaging from '@react-native-
firebase/messaging';

// Request permission for push
notifications
messaging()
  .requestPermission()
  .then(authStatus => {
    console.log('Permission status:',
authStatus);
  });

// Get the device token
messaging()
  .getToken()
  .then(token => {
    console.log('Device FCM Token:',
token);
```

```
});

// Handle incoming notifications
messaging().onMessage(async remoteMessage
=> {
    console.log('Foreground notification:',
remoteMessage);
});
```

Real-World Example: Building a Real-Time Messaging App for Mobile Devices

Let's walk through a **real-time messaging app** for mobile devices, where users can send and receive messages instantly. The app will use **WebSocket** for real-time communication and **Node.js** for the backend.

Step 1: Set Up the WebSocket Server in Node.js

We'll use **Socket.IO** to handle WebSocket connections on the server side.

```javascript
const express = require('express');
const http = require('http');
const socketIo = require('socket.io');
```

```
const app = express();
const server = http.createServer(app);
const io = socketIo(server);

io.on('connection', (socket) => {
  console.log('User connected');

  // Handle incoming messages from clients
  socket.on('sendMessage', (message) => {
    console.log('Message received:', message);
    io.emit('receiveMessage',    message);    // Broadcast the message to all clients
  });

  socket.on('disconnect', () => {
    console.log('User disconnected');
  });
});

server.listen(3000, () => {
  console.log('Server    is    running    on http://localhost:3000');
});
```

Step 2: Set Up the Mobile Client (React Native)

In the mobile app, we'll use **React Native** to connect to the WebSocket server and send/receive messages.

1. Install the **WebSocket** dependency:

```bash
npm install socket.io-client
```

2. Create a simple UI to send and display messages:

```javascript
import React, { useState, useEffect } from
'react';
import { View, Text, TextInput, Button,
FlatList } from 'react-native';
import io from 'socket.io-client';

const App = () => {
  const [message, setMessage] =
useState('');
  const [messages, setMessages] =
useState([]);
  const socket =
io('http://localhost:3000');

  useEffect(() => {
    // Listen for incoming messages
    socket.on('receiveMessage', (message)
=> {
      setMessages((prevMessages) =>
[...prevMessages, message]);
    });
```

```
    return () => {
      socket.off('receiveMessage');
    };
  }, []);

  const sendMessage = () => {
    socket.emit('sendMessage', message);
    setMessage('');
  };

  return (
    <View>
      <FlatList
        data={messages}
        renderItem={({    item    })    =>
<Text>{item}</Text>}
        keyExtractor={(item,    index)    =>
index.toString()}
      />
      <TextInput
        value={message}
        onChangeText={setMessage}
        placeholder="Type a message"
      />
      <Button                title="Send"
onPress={sendMessage} />
    </View>
  );
};
```

```
export default App;
```

Step 3: Run the App

1. Run the **Node.js WebSocket server**.
2. Open the **React Native app** on a mobile device or emulator.
3. Send messages in real-time, and all connected clients will receive them instantly.

Conclusion

In this chapter, we explored the challenges of building real-time mobile applications and how to address them using **Node.js** for backend services. We discussed:

- The difficulties faced in real-time mobile apps, including network connectivity, latency, and battery life.
- How to integrate **real-time features** like WebSockets and push notifications into mobile apps.
- A **real-world example** of building a **real-time messaging app** for mobile devices using **Node.js** and **WebSockets**.

Real-time mobile apps are becoming increasingly important in industries such as e-commerce, gaming, social media, and finance. By using technologies like **Node.js** and **WebSockets**, you can create efficient, low-latency applications that provide users with real-time interactions. In the next chapters, we will explore additional advanced topics like scaling mobile real-time apps, optimizing performance, and handling large-scale deployments.

CHAPTER 26

FUTURE OF REAL-TIME WEB APPS

Emerging Trends in Real-Time Application Development

The world of real-time web applications is continuously evolving, driven by advancements in technology and shifting user expectations. As businesses and consumers demand more seamless, immediate, and interactive experiences, real-time apps are becoming increasingly integral to various industries. Some of the emerging trends in real-time application development include:

1. **Serverless Architectures:**
   - **Serverless computing** allows developers to build and deploy applications without managing the underlying infrastructure. This reduces operational overhead and enables automatic scaling, making it easier to develop and maintain real-time applications.
   - Platforms like **AWS Lambda**, **Azure Functions**, and **Google Cloud Functions** support serverless backends, enabling real-time event-driven apps to scale effortlessly in response to demand.

2. **Edge Computing for Real-Time Processing:**

   o **Edge computing** involves processing data closer to the user's location, rather than in centralized cloud data centers. This minimizes latency and ensures that real-time applications can respond to events more quickly.

   o Real-time apps like video streaming, gaming, and IoT benefit significantly from edge computing, where data is processed on devices or at local edge servers, reducing the load on centralized servers and enhancing performance.

3. **Real-Time Data Streaming:**

   o Real-time data streaming has become more prevalent with platforms like **Apache Kafka**, **Amazon Kinesis**, and **Google Cloud Pub/Sub**. These technologies enable the efficient handling of large volumes of real-time data across distributed systems.

   o Real-time data analytics, customer behavior analysis, and live recommendations are increasingly powered by continuous data streams that provide instant insights and updates.

4. **PWA (Progressive Web Apps) for Real-Time Experiences:**

   o **Progressive Web Apps (PWAs)** offer a blend of web and mobile app capabilities, providing offline support, fast load times, and real-time capabilities like push notifications and background sync.

- o PWAs make it easier to deliver real-time experiences on both desktop and mobile without requiring users to download native apps, creating a more accessible and cost-effective solution for developers.

5. **Microservices and Event-Driven Architectures:**
   - o The adoption of **microservices** and **event-driven architectures** is accelerating the development of real-time apps, allowing for more modular, scalable, and resilient systems. Microservices help break down complex applications into smaller, independent services, which are easier to manage, update, and scale.
   - o Event-driven systems, powered by **message queues** (e.g., **RabbitMQ, Kafka**), enable real-time processing of events, ensuring that updates are handled in real time across the application.

The Role of AI and Machine Learning in Real-Time Apps

Artificial Intelligence (AI) and **Machine Learning (ML)** are transforming real-time applications by enhancing their ability to process and analyze data quickly, making dynamic decisions, and providing personalized user experiences. Some of the ways AI and ML are being integrated into real-time applications include:

1. **Personalization in Real-Time:**
   o AI can analyze user behavior in real time and dynamically adjust the content and experience based on individual preferences. For example, real-time recommendation engines in e-commerce apps suggest products based on past browsing or purchasing behavior.
   o **Collaborative filtering** and **content-based filtering** algorithms help provide tailored recommendations in real-time.

2. **Chatbots and Virtual Assistants:**
   o **AI-powered chatbots** are becoming more intelligent and capable of engaging users in natural, real-time conversations. These bots can assist with customer service, lead generation, and troubleshooting by understanding user queries and responding immediately.
   o Real-time interactions powered by AI enable users to receive responses instantly, improving satisfaction and reducing the need for human intervention.

3. **Real-Time Fraud Detection:**
   o AI and ML can analyze transactions or user activities in real-time to identify fraudulent

behavior. For example, payment systems can use **anomaly detection** algorithms to identify suspicious activity (e.g., a sudden spike in purchases) and trigger real-time alerts or block transactions.

o **Supervised learning models** can be trained on historical data to detect fraudulent patterns, while **unsupervised learning** can be used to identify previously unknown threats.

4. **Predictive Analytics:**

o Real-time predictive analytics powered by ML models can provide real-time insights into customer behavior, system performance, and trends. For example, in a retail app, machine learning algorithms can predict when a customer is most likely to make a purchase based on their browsing history and engagement patterns, prompting personalized offers in real-time.

o **Reinforcement learning** allows real-time systems to adapt and optimize based on user feedback, enhancing the performance of applications like online advertising, content delivery, and game mechanics.

5G and the Future of Real-Time Communication

5G is the next generation of mobile network technology, offering massive improvements in speed, bandwidth, and latency compared to previous generations. This makes it a game-changer for real-time applications, especially those requiring high data transfer rates and low latency.

Key Benefits of 5G for Real-Time Apps:

1. **Ultra-Low Latency:**
   o 5G promises **latencies as low as 1 millisecond**, making it ideal for real-time applications like augmented reality (AR), virtual reality (VR), remote surgery, and autonomous vehicles, where even a small delay can lead to significant problems.
   o Real-time communication apps, such as video calling and live streaming, will experience a significant reduction in lag, resulting in smoother experiences for users.

2. **Higher Data Speeds:**
   o 5G offers speeds up to **10 Gbps**, enabling the rapid transmission of high-resolution video, large files, and real-time data without interruptions.
   o Mobile apps that rely on streaming, such as gaming, video conferencing, and real-time video

307

editing, will benefit from faster data transfer rates and less buffering.

3. **Increased Network Capacity:**
   o With 5G, networks can handle significantly more devices simultaneously. This is particularly useful for IoT applications, smart cities, and mobile real-time apps that involve millions of devices communicating at once.
   o The increased capacity will allow real-time apps to scale effectively, enabling them to support millions of users without compromising performance.

4. **Edge Computing:**
   o 5G will accelerate the adoption of **edge computing**, where data processing happens closer to the user, reducing latency and ensuring faster response times for real-time apps.
   o By reducing the distance that data needs to travel, 5G will support real-time data analytics, live gaming, and other high-performance use cases.

Real-World Example: Predicting User Behavior in Real-Time with AI

Let's consider a **real-time e-commerce app** where AI is used to predict user behavior and provide personalized recommendations in real time. The app leverages both **machine learning models** and **real-time analytics** to adjust the user experience instantly based on their activity.

Step 1: Collect User Activity Data The app collects real-time data on user behavior (e.g., clicks, search history, time spent on product pages). This data is sent to the backend server and stored in a real-time database (e.g., **MongoDB** or **Redis**).

Step 2: Use Machine Learning to Analyze User Behavior Using real-time analytics, the app predicts what the user is most likely to purchase based on their recent activity. For example, an **ML recommendation model** might suggest products the user is likely to buy next.

Example Model:

- **Collaborative Filtering:** The system analyzes users with similar preferences and suggests items that others have bought.
- **Content-Based Filtering:** The app uses the products the user has shown interest in and recommends similar items based on the content (e.g., category, brand).

Step 3: Provide Real-Time Recommendations As the user interacts with the app, AI models predict what they might be interested in and push real-time notifications or in-app messages with personalized offers.

Example (Real-Time Recommendation Logic in Node.js):

javascript

```javascript
const { predictUserBehavior } = require('./mlModel'); // Load your ML model

// Endpoint to get recommendations for a user
app.get('/recommendations', async (req, res) => {
  const userId = req.query.userId;
  const userActivity = await getUserActivity(userId); // Fetch recent activity

  const predictions = predictUserBehavior(userActivity);
  res.json({ recommendations: predictions });
});

// ML Model Function (simplified):
function predictUserBehavior(activityData) {
  // Use a trained ML model to predict the products the user will likely buy
  const recommendations = activityData.map(product => {
    return { productId: product.id, score: Math.random() }; // Simulated model output
  });
  return recommendations;
```

}

Step 4: Send Real-Time Notifications The app sends real-time **push notifications** or **in-app messages** based on the AI predictions. For instance, if a user is likely to buy a particular product, they may receive a limited-time discount offer for that product.

Step 5: Continuous Feedback and Learning The model continues to learn from real-time data, refining its predictions based on user interactions. This continuous feedback loop helps improve the accuracy of recommendations over time.

Conclusion

In this chapter, we explored the **future of real-time web applications** and how emerging trends like AI, **5G**, and **serverless architectures** are shaping the landscape. We covered:

- The increasing role of **AI and machine learning** in enhancing real-time experiences through personalized content, predictive analytics, and real-time decision-making.
- The transformative impact of **5G** on real-time applications, especially in reducing latency and enabling

high-speed, high-capacity communication for mobile apps.

- A **real-world example** of **predicting user behavior in real time** using machine learning in an c-commerce application.

As technology continues to advance, the potential for real-time web apps will only expand, offering more personalized, interactive, and seamless experiences. The next chapters will focus on practical implementations of these emerging trends, exploring how to integrate AI, 5G, and real-time analytics into your apps to deliver cutting-edge functionality and performance.

CHAPTER 27

CONCLUSION AND NEXT STEPS

Summarizing the Journey of Building Real-Time Apps with Node.js

Throughout this book, we've explored the exciting and dynamic world of **real-time web applications** built with **Node.js**. From understanding the fundamentals of WebSockets and APIs to diving into advanced topics like WebRTC, microservices, and integrating AI for real-time personalization, we've covered the essential tools, patterns, and best practices required to develop scalable and efficient real-time applications.

Here's a quick recap of the journey:

1. **Introduction to Real-Time Web Apps:**
    o We started by laying the foundation, exploring the unique characteristics of real-time web applications, and understanding why Node.js is an excellent choice for building such apps.
2. **WebSockets and Real-Time Communication:**
    o We delved into **WebSockets**, learning how to establish persistent, low-latency communication between clients and servers, which is critical for

313

real-time features like live chats, notifications, and data streaming.

3. **Building Real-Time Applications:**
   o We built a simple real-time chat app, learned about asynchronous programming, and explored how to scale real-time applications using Node.js.

4. **Advanced Real-Time Features:**
   o As we moved forward, we explored complex real-time features like **real-time audio and video streaming** (via **WebRTC**) and **integrating WebSockets with real-time databases** like Redis, MongoDB, and Kafka for event-driven applications.

5. **Security and Optimization:**
   o Securing WebSocket connections, protecting real-time apps from **DDoS attacks**, and implementing **end-to-end encryption** for sensitive data were also critical aspects we covered.

6. **Mobile Real-Time Apps:**
   o We learned how to implement real-time features in mobile apps using technologies like **React Native**, along with best practices for handling mobile-specific challenges like connectivity and battery life.

7. **Real-Time Analytics and Monitoring:**

  o The importance of **real-time monitoring dashboards, analytics** for user behavior, and integrating **AI and machine learning** for predictive analytics were explored in detail.

8. **Deployment and Scaling:**

  o The deployment of real-time applications was covered using **Docker, Kubernetes,** and cloud platforms like AWS to ensure scalability and high availability.

9. **Future Trends:**

  o We concluded by looking ahead at **emerging trends** in real-time development, including the role of **5G, AI,** and **edge computing,** and how these technologies will impact the future of real-time web apps.

Key Takeaways and Best Practices

Here are some of the key takeaways and best practices for building real-time web applications:

1. **Use WebSockets for Low-Latency, Bi-Directional Communication:**

  o For real-time features like messaging, notifications, or live updates, WebSockets are a must. They provide persistent, bi-directional communication with low overhead.

2. **Security is Essential:**
   o Real-time apps must prioritize **data security**. Always use **WSS** for WebSocket connections, authenticate users using **JWT**, and ensure end-to-end encryption for sensitive data.

3. **Scalability:**
   o Real-time apps need to be designed for scalability. Use load balancing, **horizontal scaling**, and distributed architectures like **microservices** to ensure that your app can handle growth in traffic and users.

4. **Optimize Performance and Latency:**
   o Optimize network requests and data transmission for minimal latency. Use **CDNs**, **caching**, and **edge computing** to improve speed and responsiveness for global users.

5. **Monitor and Analyze in Real-Time:**
   o Integrating **real-time monitoring** and **analytics** into your app allows you to track user behavior, monitor performance, and detect issues proactively.

6. **Leverage Cloud Services and Containerization:**

- o Tools like **AWS, Docker,** and **Kubernetes** are essential for deploying scalable, resilient, and high-availability real-time applications.

7. **Experiment with AI and Machine Learning:**
   - o Use AI and ML for personalized recommendations, real-time fraud detection, and predictive analytics. These technologies add a layer of intelligence that can elevate the user experience.

How to Continue Learning and Exploring Real-Time Web Development

While this book has provided a strong foundation in building real-time web applications, the field of real-time development is constantly evolving. Here are some ways to continue learning and exploring:

1. **Stay Updated with New Technologies:**
   - o Follow industry blogs, documentation, and GitHub repositories for the latest advancements in real-time frameworks, such as WebSockets, **gRPC,** and **GraphQL Subscriptions.**

2. **Explore New Real-Time Use Cases:**
   - o Experiment with new real-time application scenarios like **augmented reality (AR), virtual**

reality (VR), IoT devices, and live data feeds that rely on real-time processing.

3. **Join Communities and Contribute:**
   o Join developer communities like Stack Overflow, GitHub, and Reddit to collaborate with other developers, contribute to open-source projects, and get feedback on your real-time app ideas.

4. **Take Advanced Courses:**
   o Consider enrolling in specialized courses or certifications on platforms like **Udemy**, **Coursera**, or **Pluralsight** that offer deeper dives into advanced real-time development topics.

5. **Practice Building and Scaling Real-Time Apps:**
   o Continuously build and scale more complex real-time apps. Practice handling edge cases, optimizing for performance, and incorporating advanced features like **AI-powered chatbots** or **real-time analytics dashboards**.

Final Real-World Example: Launching Your Own Scalable Real-Time Web App

Let's take everything we've learned and apply it to a **real-world project**: **Building and launching a scalable real-time messaging app**. Here's a step-by-step guide to get you started:

1. **Define the Core Features:**
   o The messaging app should support:
     - Real-time messaging with WebSockets.
     - User authentication (e.g., JWT-based).
     - Push notifications for new messages.
     - Real-time typing indicators and status updates.

2. **Back-End Setup:**
   o Use **Node.js** with **Socket.IO** for real-time messaging.
   o Store messages and user data in a **MongoDB** database.
   o Secure WebSocket connections with **WSS** and implement **JWT authentication**.

3. **Front-End Setup:**
   o Build the front end using **React** or **React Native** for mobile apps.
   o Use **WebSocket** to establish real-time communication.
   o Integrate **Push Notifications** using Firebase for mobile apps.

4. **Deployment and Scaling:**
   o Containerize the app using **Docker**.
   o Use **Kubernetes** for orchestration and **AWS** or **Google Cloud** for hosting.

- o Implement **auto-scaling** and **load balancing** to handle high traffic.

5. **Monitoring and Analytics:**
   - o Set up **real-time monitoring** using **Prometheus** and **Grafana**.
   - o Implement **logging** and **error tracking** to monitor application health and troubleshoot issues in real time.

6. **Launch:**
   - o After testing and ensuring the app's scalability, security, and performance, deploy it to the cloud, monitor user behavior in real time, and iterate based on feedback.

By following these steps, you can build a robust, scalable real-time web application and launch it for your users, ensuring a seamless, interactive experience with real-time features.

Conclusion

In this final chapter, we've summarized the journey of building real-time applications with **Node.js**, from understanding the basic concepts to implementing complex real-time features like WebSockets, push notifications, and AI-powered analytics. We've explored best practices, security measures, and scalability

320

techniques that are essential for building robust and scalable real-time web apps.

As you move forward, continue experimenting, learning, and applying these concepts to new projects. The field of real-time web development is dynamic, and there are always new tools and technologies emerging that can enhance your applications and the user experience.

Good luck with your real-time development journey!